THE A-TECH CORPORATION PRESENTS

BE PRACTICAL

THE ONLY HANDBOOK YOU NEED TO OWN AI IN YOUR BUSINESS.

HAMISH AMAN PRAKASH

ATG
PUBLISHING

BE PRACTICAL: The only Handbook you NEED to OWN AI in your business.

For information contact :

ATG Publishing

info@atgpublishing.com - http://www.atgpublishing.com

ISBN: 9781991123046

First Edition: December 2025

10 9 8 7 6 5 4 3 2 1

CONTENTS

DEDICATIONS

The Prakash Family from Waila and Nausori Fiji.

When my family left Fiji in the mid-80s due to the countless Coops from the military, it wasn't easy to begin life again. They started from the bottom and brought me up to the point where I could be privileged enough to be able to explore the fascinating world of AI, robotics and emerging technologies. When I got seriously unwell you were all there for me when I needed you all the most.

Madeleine P. You were my first ever client all the way back in 2021. Thank you for putting your trust in me.

Rhadika N. Whenever I was feeling like giving up, you always reminded me why I shouldn't. And I'll love you forever as a result of it

Morgan M. You're the reason why I'm here today my bro. Thank you for being by my side in the early days. You're the man!

All our past, present and future clients & partners. Without you none of this would have been possible. Thank you for trusting A-Tech.

A Quick, Honest Word

I'm going to make this really practical for you, because that's what this book is about: being practical. Everything I've shared in these pages—the strategies, the stories of how AI saved my business, the path to owning your tools—is 100% real and based on my experience in the trenches. But here's the thing: Your business is not my business. Your resources are not my resources.

The world of AI is also changing so fast that what's cutting-edge today might be old news by the time you read this.

This book is your roadmap, not your GPS. It shows you the destination and the best possible routes I've found, but you are still the one who has to drive the car.

What This Book Is NOT:

A Magic Bullet: This book is not promising a magic bullet or an instant fix for your business. AI is powerful, but it is not effortless. Building useful AI systems takes time, curiosity, learning, and a willingness to solve problems along the way. There will be moments where things do not work perfectly the first time, and that is part of the process.

That said, when AI is implemented thoughtfully and aligned to real business needs, the results can be genuinely transformative. The approach in this book is practical and hands-on, designed to help you build solutions that are tailored to how your business actually operates, not generic tools that only work in theory.

This book focuses on the do-it-yourself path, giving you the understanding and confidence to build and own your own AI solutions. If you would prefer a faster, more turnkey option, ready-to-use AI systems are also available through A-Tech. Either way, the goal remains the same: using AI in a practical way to support, strengthen, and improve your business.

Legal or Financial Advice: I'm an entrepreneur who has used AI to solve problems, not a lawyer or an accountant. The ideas and frameworks here are for educational purposes. When it comes to implementing these strategies—especially regarding data privacy, customer contracts, and major financial decisions—please consult qualified professionals who understand your specific situation.

A Guarantee of Results: I believe these principles can transform your business because they transformed mine. However, I cannot guarantee you will achieve the exact same outcomes. Your success will depend on your commitment, your unique business context, and how you apply these ideas.

What This Book IS

A Proven Framework: A practical, step-by-step guide to thinking about and implementing AI in a way that builds real business value.

A Catalyst for Action: My goal is to demystify AI and give you the confidence and the tools to start today. The biggest risk isn't trying something and failing; it's doing nothing while your competitors move ahead.

A Foundation for Ownership: This is your starting point for building a business that isn't dependent on you—or on expensive monthly subscriptions. It's the first step toward freedom. Think back to when OpenAI launched ChatGPT-5 and turned off the older models in 2025. Which caused chaos.

My challenge to you is to take these ideas, adapt them to your world, and start small. Test one thing. Learn from it. Then test another.

The journey to owning your AI starts not with a giant leap, but with that first, practical step.

Now, let's get to work.

Introduction: Welcome to Practical AI

The noise surrounding Artificial Intelligence is deafening these days, isn't it? You hear it everywhere - boardroom whispers, headlines screaming disruption, consultants promising the moon. You see competitors making moves, dabbling in things that sound impossibly complex, and you feel that nagging pressure: "Am I keeping up? What should **I** be doing?"

You've likely asked yourself, "How do I actually use this stuff in **my** business, without needing a PhD in computer science or remortgaging the office?" It's a fair question. Perhaps you've seen the eye-watering price tags some consultancies charge and thought, "There has to be a better way." Or maybe you've tried dipping your toe into the vast ocean of AI information online, only to drown in jargon and waste precious hours.

Here's the thing: while you're spending all that time just trying to get your head around it, your competitors might already be five steps ahead. They could be streamlining processes, understanding customers better, making smarter decisions – all powered by the very technology that feels just out of your reach.

That gap between AI's potential and practical reality for most businesses? **That** is precisely why this book exists.

I felt this wasn't just important to write; it was **necessary**. We needed something straightforward, honest, something a busy business owner could pick up and immediately understand **how** to implement AI in their specific context. No fluff, no impenetrable theory, just practical steps you can take today. This isn't another theoretical treatise destined to gather dust. It's your handbook, your journal, your **action plan** – designed to cut through the noise and make AI accessible, understandable, and most importantly, **actionable** for **your** business, right now.

WHO AM I TO GUIDE YOU?

My name is Hamish. I'm an entrepreneur with multiple businesses, YouTube channels, and countless reasons to stay in bed some mornings. I'm the founder of The A-Tech Corporation, based in Queensland - we became the first AI studio in our region in 2023. We've worked with governments, nonprofits, small to medium businesses, brick and mortar, digital and many more. Think of us less as a tech company and more as a practical consulting firm rooted in the real world. While we can solve complex problems, our focus is on providing clarity and strategy - solutions that businesses like yours can actually implement themselves.

But that's not really why I wrote this book.

The real reason is much more personal. And it starts with a diagnosis that changed everything...

HOW AI SAVED MY BUSINESS (AND MY LIFE)

I want to share something personal with you. Something I don't talk about often, but it's actually the reason I'm so passionate about AI and automation.

I have something called Functional Neurological Disorder (FND). What that means is:

- I experience seizures that can happen without warning
- I can't straighten my right hand
- I can't walk for more than 3-4 minutes without triggering my symptoms

Some days are good, some days are really tough and I can't even roll out of bed.

Before you feel sorry for me, let me tell you: This condition ended up being one of the best things that ever happened to my business.

The Breaking Point

There was a time when my health got really bad. I was trying to run my business the "normal" way - being in the office every day, meeting clients, managing a team, doing all the things business owners are "supposed" to do.

But my body had other plans. I'd be in the middle of an important meeting and suddenly need to leave because a seizure was starting. I'd try to work a full day but be exhausted after 20 minutes. I'd plan my week perfectly, then wake up unable to get out of bed.

I remember lying in bed one night thinking: "I can't do this anymore. I'm going to have to give up my business."

The AI Awakening

That's when it hit me. If I couldn't work like everyone else, maybe I didn't have to. Maybe I could build a business that worked for me.

I started asking different questions:

Instead of "How can I work more hours?" I asked, "How can my business work without me?"

Instead of "How can I meet more clients?" I asked, "How can AI help clients without me being there?"

Instead of "How can I manage my team better?" I asked, "How can systems manage everything automatically?"

Building My AI Business

I went all in on AI and automation. Here's what I built:

AI That Handles Clients: Instead of me personally answering every question, I built AI systems that could handle 80-90% of client communications. They know my business, my style, my solutions. They can help clients 24/7, even when I'm sleeping or having a seizure.

Automated Workflows: I created systems that handle everything - sales, onboarding, project management, billing - without me touching anything. If a new client signs up at 2 AM, the system welcomes them, sets up their account, and gets them started, even if I'm in bed unable to move.

AI-Powered Decision Making: I built tools that analyze business data and tell me what needs attention. Instead of me spending hours looking at numbers, the AI says "Hey, you need to focus on this today" or "This project is going off track."

The Results Shocked Me

Within a few months, my business was running better than ever before. But here's the crazy part - I was working LESS, not more.

My clients were happier because they got instant responses. My revenue went up because the systems never missed opportunities. My stress went down because I wasn't constantly worried about having a seizure during an important meeting.

Health and Business Working Together

Here's what most people don't understand: Building an AI-powered business didn't just help me make money. It helped me stay healthy.

When I have a bad day health-wise, my business keeps running. The AI handles client calls, the automation keeps projects moving, the systems keep making money.

When I have a good day health-wise, I can focus on the things that really matter - big picture strategy, creative work, the parts of the business that actually need human thinking.

I'm not forced to push through pain just to keep the lights on anymore. My business works with my health, not against it.

Why This Matters for You

You might not have FND. You might be perfectly healthy. But here's what I learned that applies to every business owner:

Life Happens: You might get sick, have a family emergency, face a personal crisis, or just need a vacation. If your business depends on you being there 24/7, you're one bad day away from disaster.

Freedom is the Goal: The real reason to build an AI-powered business isn't just to make more money. It's to build a life where you don't have to choose between your health and your business.

Systems Beat Hustle: Working 80 hours a week isn't a badge of honor. It's a sign that your systems aren't working. Smart AI systems can outperform hustle every single time.

My Challenge to You

Look at your business right now. If you couldn't work for a week, what would happen? Would everything fall apart? Or would your systems keep things running?

If the answer is "everything would fall apart," then you don't have a business - you have a job that owns you.

Building AI systems isn't just about technology or efficiency. It's about building a business that gives you freedom, flexibility, and control over your life.

For me, AI didn't just save my business. It gave me my life back. And I believe it can do the same for you, whatever challenges you're facing.

The question isn't whether you'll face challenges in life and business. The question is whether you'll build systems that can handle those challenges for you.

That's the real power of AI ownership. It's not just about technology - it's about building a life and business that works for you, no matter what life throws your way.

That life-changing experience taught me more about business than any MBA ever could - starting with the most fundamental question every business owner needs to answer:

What does AI mean for my business?

Cutting Through the Noise – What AI Really Means for Your Business

We know why we're here. We want to understand AI and how it helps our business.

But what IS AI, really? When you ignore the hype, scary news stories, and wild predictions, what does AI mean for YOUR business, YOUR team, and more importantly… YOUR money?

I get this question a lot. People ask:

- Is AI just a fancy new tool?
- Is it like having a super-smart assistant?
- Will robots take all our jobs?

You hear experts talk about AI that might become smarter than people, and it's easy to worry. "What does this mean for my sales goals this month?"

Here's the truth: For your business today, AI can be all those things - a tool, an assistant, and yes, it might do some jobs people do now. But this will happen slowly. The idea of replacing your entire team tomorrow?

Probably not going to happen. Maybe in two years things will look different - technology moves fast.

But what does super-smart AI mean for YOUR business right now? In terms of problems? Honestly? Not much. Don't let scary future stories stop you from moving forward today.

However,... and this is BIG... the opportunity to use AI to HELP your business? That potential is INCREDIBLE, starting TODAY. But only if you use it the right way. And that "right way" is exactly what this book will teach you.

So, forget the complicated tech talk. Let's focus on what AI can DO and how it helps YOUR business make more money.

Think about it like this:

Can AI help you identify customers who may be considering leaving your product or service early? YES

Can AI read customer feedback faster than a person? YES

Can AI write first drafts of ads or social media posts? YES

Can AI handle boring data entry better than old computer rules? YES

These are the real things AI can do for your business right now. Not tomorrow - TODAY.

The secret isn't to worry about AI taking over the world. The secret is to use AI as your assistant to solve real problems and make your business stronger. That's what we'll explore together in this book.

AI VS. AUTOMATION VS. ALGORITHMS – GETTING THE FOUNDATIONS RIGHT

This section might be the most important one in this whole book. Why? Because I see so many people get confused, and that confusion costs them money and missed chances.

Business owners tell me, "I wish AI could do everything for me!" Then I look at their business and find they're already using smart tools like Zapier to connect their software. They have email filters that sort their messages automatically. They have systems that run like clockwork.

The funny part? They don't even realize they're already using automation and algorithms - the building blocks of AI! They hear "AI" and think of robots, missing that smart automation may already be helping them, or that adding AI to what they already do could be their next big step.

So why is this important for you to understand?

To remain competitive and relevant in an increasingly automated world, grasping the fundamentals of AI is no longer optional—it is a critical imperative for the modern business leader. This handbook is designed to cut through the noise and provide the pragmatic, actionable knowledge necessary to demystify AI and immediately integrate its power into your operational reality. By understanding the principles outlined here, you will not just observe the future of business; you will actively shape it, ensuring your enterprise is built for efficiency, innovation, and sustained success.

Let's break this down simply:

ALGORITHMS

Think of these as recipes. They're step-by-step instructions that always work the same way. If you do X, then Y happens. Simple and clear.

Humans have used algorithms forever! From library book systems to pilot checklists to how you pay bills - these are all algorithms. Businesses have used them for hundreds of years.

Automation

This is when you use technology to run those recipes automatically, without people having to do them over and over.

Think about your accounting software that sends reminder emails when bills are 14 days late. That's automation following a simple rule: (IF the bill is 14 days late AND not paid, THEN send a reminder email).

Tools like Zapier are great at this - they connect different apps using triggers and actions.

Artificial Intelligence (AI):

The truth is, AI isn't some futuristic, silver-bullet solution arriving on a spaceship. It's a pragmatic, highly adaptable toolset, a sophisticated form of automation for knowledge work. Think of it as the most powerful, diligent intern you could ever hire—one that can process mountains of data, write coherent first drafts, and identify patterns invisible to the naked eye. It operates on logic, probability, and vast datasets, stripping away the guesswork and emotion from decision-making. AI isn't magic; it's just efficiency, codified. The goal isn't to replace human intelligence, but to augment it, handling the tedious and complex so that your team can focus on strategy, creativity, and the human element that truly drives a business forward.

This is where things get smarter. AI goes beyond fixed rules. It can:

- Learn from data
- Change its answers
- Handle unclear situations
- Make predictions
- Spot complex patterns
- Create new content (like writing text)

Think about ChatGPT. At its core, it only understands computer code (ones and zeros). So how can we talk to it using language we use with others? Because we trained it on lots of human language using smart algorithms and automation systems. See how they work together? AI needs algorithms and automation to exist.

What This Means for Your Business:

Understanding this difference helps you pick the right tools.

You may already be using AI directly:

- A chatbot for customer service
- A tool that predicts sales
- ChatGPT to write emails

Then, you could add AI to your Automation:

- Imagine your current Zapier workflow
- Add an AI step to check if customer feedback is happy or upset
- Have AI summarize long documents before sending them to your team

You may then build AI into Algorithms for custom solutions:

- This is where things get exciting
- Create special tools that use AI to make business processes better

Here's a real example: I worked with a business that struggled to find their perfect customers. They usually paid marketing agencies lots of money for this. In less than 30 minutes, I built a simple AI tool.

They just entered basic info: what their business does, who they want to reach, age groups, where they post online. The tool created detailed customer profiles they could use right away in their marketing.

Simple idea, built with AI algorithms, but incredibly powerful and saved them money. Suddenly, the "impossible" became possible.

Let's be clear: Is an email filter that sends all messages with "invoice" in the subject to your accounting department AI? No - that's automation following a simple rule.

But is a spam filter that LEARNS over time what YOU think is junk mail, even if it doesn't have obvious spam words? THAT'S closer to AI, because it learns and recognizes patterns.

Knowing the difference stops you from paying for "AI" when simple automation works fine. It also helps you spot where real AI could make your current systems much better.

Dodging the Landmines – Choosing the Right AI System for You

We've learned what AI really is. Now comes the question I hear every single day: **"Which AI should I use?"**

Honestly, there are so many choices out there, it can feel like walking through a minefield blindfolded. And here's what I see happen all the time:

A business owner comes to me looking stressed, listing all the software they're juggling: "I have this tool for customers, another one for emails, another for projects, this one for numbers, and that one for social media... Can I just plug AI into everything and make it all talk to each other?"

My first thought isn't about AI at all. It's: "Wait - do you really NEED all those tools?"

Before you even think about adding AI, you MUST look honestly at what you're already using. The truth is, most businesses have too many overlapping tools they don't really need. They're trying to do simple jobs with a complicated mess of software.

Think about building a tower with wooden blocks. You keep adding more blocks - new tools, new subscriptions - hoping to reach higher. But if the base isn't solid, or if you're adding blocks you don't need, what happens? The tower gets wobbly and eventually falls over.

Adding AI to an already messy tech stack is like adding heavy blocks to the top of a shaky tower. It just makes things worse.

Remember our goal: We want AI to make us MORE efficient, MORE streamlined, and maybe save money or time. We don't want to add another expensive subscription just to say "we're doing AI."

So Step Zero before choosing any AI is: Look at what you already have. Ask yourself honestly:

1. What does each tool actually do?
2. Do any tools do the same job?
3. If I get an AI tool for Task X, can I finally get rid of that OTHER tool I was using for Task X?

Be tough. Cut what you don't need. Simplify.

Finding Your Way Through the AI Maze

Okay, now that you've audited and cleaned up your current tools, we can talk about choosing AI. But it's not about picking a famous brand name. It's about understanding what YOU need.

Here are three big questions to answer:

1. The Privacy Question: Keep It Private or Use the Cloud?

Is your data highly sensitive, requiring the AI to operate solely on your internal infrastructure instead of a cloud-based environment for maximum privacy and safety?

Or are you okay with the fact your data might be processed somewhere else using cloud AI tools like ChatGPT?

The trade-off is usually privacy vs. getting the newest features without managing the tech yourself. There's no right answer - it depends on your business rules, how sensitive your data is, and what matters most to you.

2. The Problem Question: What Are You Trying to Fix?

AI isn't magic you sprinkle over your whole business. You need to be specific. Where will you use it FIRST?

Marketing and Content? Making pictures, writing ads, checking how campaigns work?

Sales and Office Work? Building AI phone assistants, sending follow-up emails, smart chatbots that talk to thousands of customers?

Operations or HR? Finding problems in how things work, helping with hiring, generating custom reports automatically?

The AI that's great for sales numbers is very different from the AI that writes creative ads. Knowing your main problem helps you choose the right tool.

3. The Partnership Question: AI That Does It All or AI That Helps You?

How do you want to work WITH AI? There are two main ways:

Full Autonomy

You give AI a big job (maybe thousands of steps), and it works by itself, figuring out how to do everything. Think of AI researching for your business while you focus on more important things. These systems might take hours or even a day, but they can handle huge, complex jobs alone.

Human + AI Team

This is what most businesses use today. You use AI tools like ChatGPT as super-smart assistants. AI speeds up the work - writing drafts, summarizing reports, handling boring data entry - but you stay in control. You guide the AI, check its work, and make the final decisions. You become less of a worker and more of a director, using AI to make yourself more powerful.

Understanding these three questions - Privacy, Problem, and Partnership - moves you from "I need AI" to knowing exactly what KIND of AI fits your business.

The Big Question: Cost

I mentioned this before, and it's important: choosing wrong can be **expensive**. Jumping into a private AI system that costs more upfront but has no monthly fees, when a cloud tool would work but can burn through money fast.

The key is matching your choice to what you actually need, not what sounds exciting.

Can You Do This Yourself? Or Do You Need Help?

How technical are you?

Could you navigate this selection process and implement AI yourself, or do you need to hire an agency or a consulting firm like ours? The honest answer is: it depends.

For simpler, off-the-shelf tools addressing common problems, many businesses can manage the selection and basic implementation themselves, especially using frameworks like the Needs Assessment.

However, for more complex integrations, custom solutions, or strategic guidance on navigating the rapidly changing landscape, expert help can save you significant time, money, and headaches in the long run.

We'll touch more on making this decision later, but the frameworks in this book are designed to empower you as much as possible, regardless of the path you choose.

The Art of the Ask – Talking to Your AI

This is another important aspect of this book. How you talk to or interact with AI is the one skill that unlocks AI's true power. Forget fancy code or complex math. We're talking about using your words. We call this **Prompt Engineering** - learning how to talk to AI using plain English.

Some of you might think, "Talking to a computer? How hard can it be?" But there's a huge difference between vaguely requesting something and giving clear instructions that get you exactly what you need.

Honestly, if you remember only one thing from this book, make it the principles I'm about to teach you. Why? Because mastering this skill is like getting a superpower in today's business world.

Right now, AI tools like ChatGPT can write, analyze, code, plan, and create. They're incredibly powerful engines. But like any engine, they need fuel and direction. Your prompt is that fuel and direction.

Get this right, and YOU - the business owner, the manager, the person working alone - can do things that used to need a whole team of people. I'm not kidding. Someone who masters prompt engineering can do the work of 100 full-time workers. That's how powerful this is. It turns AI from a cool toy into a super-powered extension of yourself.

The Main Rule: Good In, Good Out

The secret isn't really a secret. It's the same thing you already know from managing people: **clear instructions matter.**

Think about telling someone on your team what to do. If you give vague instructions, what happens? You get results that miss the mark, need lots of changes, and waste everyone's time. You can have the most powerful AI in the world, but if you don't know how to talk to it, you might as well be shouting into the void. The quality of your AI's output is almost entirely dependent on the quality of your input. This is the single most important skill you will develop on this journey.

Using AI with a bad prompt is like asking a brilliant expert for help but giving them no context, no instructions, and no idea what you're trying to achieve. You'll get a vague, unhelpful answer. A great prompt is like giving that same expert a perfectly written brief. They'll deliver exactly what you need, every time.

These AI tools are amazing, but they can't read your mind. They work with what you tell them. Vague prompts give vague answers. Clear, well-structured prompts give clear, useful, and often surprisingly good answers.

Answer This for Me

Be honest with yourself. How clearly do you usually tell your human team what to do? Are your instructions crystal clear, or sometimes rushed and unclear? Now think about how that might work when you start "telling" an AI what to do.

Knowing yourself is the first step to becoming better at giving instructions.

Crafting Effective Business Prompts: A Structured Approach

Moving from vague requests to precise, powerful instructions is the key to unlocking the full potential of AI in a business context. A well-crafted prompt acts as a clear blueprint, guiding the AI to produce exactly the output you need. While advanced techniques exist, mastering a fundamental structure will dramatically improve your results.

The most effective prompts are built on four core components: Role, Task, Specifics, and Examples. Let's break down each element.

1. Role: Assign the AI an Identity

What it is: The Role tells the AI who it should be. By assigning a persona, you tap into a specific subset of its training data, shaping its vocabulary, perspective, and depth of knowledge.

Why it works: An AI doesn't have a single identity; it's a blend of countless sources. Defining a role focuses its "mind" and sets the professional context for the entire interaction. It's the difference between getting a generic answer and getting advice from a virtual expert.

Examples of Roles:
"Act as a seasoned Chief Financial Officer."

"You are a customer success specialist with 10 years of experience in SaaS."

"Assume the role of a creative brand strategist."

"Be a meticulous project manager specializing in Agile methodologies."

2. Task: Define the Action Clearly

What it is: The Task is the core action verb. It tells the AI what you want it to do, using a direct and unambiguous command.

Why it works: A clear task eliminates guesswork. Instead of hinting at a topic, you are issuing a direct instruction. This focuses the AI's computational energy on executing a specific function, leading to more relevant and structured outputs.

Examples of Tasks:

"Analyze the following customer feedback data..."

"Draft a formal proposal for..."

"Summarize the key takeaways from this article..."

"Generate five distinct marketing slogans for..."

"Compare the pros and cons of..."

3. Specifics: Provide the Guardrails and Details

What it is: Specifics are the crucial details that shape the final output. This is where you provide the context, constraints, and formatting instructions that guide the how. This component often includes several sub-elements.

Why it works: Specifics prevent the AI from making incorrect assumptions. They act as guardrails, ensuring the response is not only accurate but also perfectly tailored to your audience, format, and goals.

Key Elements of Specifics:

Context & Goal: What is the background information? Who is the audience? What is the ultimate purpose of this content?

***Example*:** "The audience is our executive leadership team. The goal is to secure a budget for Q4."

Format: How should the response be structured?

***Example*:** "Provide the answer in a three-column table," "Use bullet points for each feature," "Write this as a formal email."

Tone & Style: What is the desired voice and personality?

***Example*:** "Use a confident and professional tone," "Write in a friendly, approachable style," "The language should be highly technical and precise."

Constraints: What are the rules, limitations, or inclusions? ***Example***: "Keep the response under 200 words," "Do not mention our competitors by name," "You must include the phrase 'synergistic solutions'."

4. Examples: Show, Don't Just Tell

What it is: Examples provide a concrete model of the desired output. This can be done in two ways: by comparing a bad prompt to a good one (as we do here), or by providing a sample input/output pair directly within the prompt (known as few-shot prompting).

Why it works: Examples are one of the most powerful ways to align the AI's understanding with your own. They remove ambiguity about style, structure, and content, giving the AI a clear target to aim for.

Example of an In-Prompt Example (Few-Shot): "Translate the following customer inquiries into a formal, professional tone.

Example 1: *Customer:* 'Hey, my stuff is broken, when will it be fixed?' *Formal Tone:* 'I am writing to report an issue with my recent order. Could you please provide an estimated timeline for the resolution?'

Example 2: *Customer:* 'I can't find the download link for my purchase.' *Formal Tone:* 'I am unable to locate the download link for my recent purchase. Could you please assist me by providing access?' Now, translate this inquiry: *Customer:* 'My invoice is wrong, you overcharged me.'"

Putting It All Together: A Business Case Study

Let's see how this framework transforms a vague request into a high-precision instruction.

Bad Prompt: "Write an email about our new service." (This prompt lacks a Role, has a vague Task, and provides zero Specifics.)

Good Prompt (using the R-T-S-E framework):

Role: "Act as our Senior Sales Manager."

Task: "Draft a professional email to our current enterprise-level customers announcing our new 'AI Strategy Check' service."

Specifics:

- **Context/Goal:** "The goal is to drive bookings for introductory meetings. The audience consists of long-term clients who trust our expertise."
- **Format:** "A short email, under 150 words, with a clear subject line."
- **Tone:** "Confident, value-focused, and consultative."
- **Constraints:** "You must highlight the main benefit: 'identifying

immediate cost-saving opportunities with AI.' Include a clear call-to-action to book a free 15-minute discovery call using this link: [link]."

Examples: (Not required here but could be added for highly specific stylistic needs.)

See the difference? The second prompt provides a complete, unambiguous blueprint, empowering the AI to generate a high-quality, ready-to-use business asset on the first try.

From Conversation to Automation: Zero-Shot Prompting

You will interact with AI in two primary ways. The first is **conversational**, where you refine the output through a series of back-and-forth questions. This is ideal for brainstorming and exploration.

The second, more critical for business automation, is **zero-shot prompting**. This means writing a single, comprehensive prompt (like the "Good Prompt" above) that contains all necessary instructions for the AI to get it right on the first try, without any follow-up. Mastering the **Role, Task, Specifics, Examples** framework is the key to effective zero-shot prompting, ensuring consistency and reliability in automated workflows.

Your Go-To Prompt Template

To build consistently effective prompts, especially for automation, use this structured template:

Role: (Who should the AI be?)
Task: (What specific action should it perform?)
Specifics:
  Context/Goal: (What's the background and purpose?)
  Audience: (Who is this for?)
  Format: (How should the output be structured?)
  Tone: (What voice should it use?)
  Constraints: (What are the rules, word counts, or required phrases?)
Examples: (Can you provide a sample of the desired output?)

By adopting this structured approach, you will transform your AI from a generic chatbot into a specialized, reliable, and highly effective business assistant.

The Human Element - Training Your Team to Thrive with AI

Let's talk about something important. Here's a truth you need to know: Your team is probably already using AI.

Yes, really. Tools like ChatGPT and others. They're using them to write emails, brainstorm ideas, maybe even summarize reports. And why haven't they told you?

Plain and simple... Fear!

They're often scared that admitting to using these tools will make you angry. They worry you'll think they're cheating, being lazy, or worse - that you'll see them as replaceable and fire them. So they keep it quiet, feeling guilty and unsure.

If you're a manager, how you react to this is super important. It might decide whether AI helps your business grow or becomes a source of worry and missed chances.

If your first reaction is anger or wanting to ban AI - stop. Take a deep breath. Because if you punish or fire people who are trying new tools to do their jobs better, you're making a huge mistake.

These aren't lazy workers. These are likely your best, most forward-thinking team members. They're trying to find ways to work better and faster FOR THEMSELVES, and then ultimately FOR YOU.

They want to make their jobs easier so they can give you better results, handle more work, or focus on important things. You need to see it that way and tell your team that's how you see it.

Your first, most important job is to make AI normal and okay. This isn't a "soft" initiative; it's a strategic imperative. The single biggest barrier to AI adoption in any organization is not the technology itself, but the human response to it. Fear, uncertainty, and doubt will stall progress far more effectively than any technical limitation. Before you can train your team on how to use AI, you must create an environment where they are psychologically willing and eager to do so.

Think back to the introduction of the internet or the PC into the workplace. There was initial skepticism, fear of obsolescence, and confusion about the "right" way to use them. Leaders who embraced these technologies openly and created clear use-cases surged ahead, while those who ignored or feared them were left behind. AI is the next great technological shift, and your leadership in normalizing its use is the critical first step.

Have you or your leaders talk about it openly. Create a place where trying new things is good (within smart limits, of course). Make it crystal clear: **"It's okay to use AI here. Your job is safe. We want to learn how these tools can help us together."**

If you can't get that message across, the rest of this book might be difficult. Because making AI work isn't just about technology - it's about people. You need to get the people part right first.

Why bother? The Huge Benefits You Can't Ignore

For leaders ready to embrace this change, think about the good things. We're seeing AI handle big parts - let's say 75-80% - of many routine tasks in office work, sales help, marketing, and daily business.

If a tool can do most of those boring, time-consuming tasks, freeing your team for smarter work, better customer talks, or new ideas... why wouldn't you want to try it? Fighting against AI is like making your team dig with spoons when you have a backhoe available.

Your team members, especially the ones already trying AI, want help. They're in new territory and need:

Clear Rules: What's okay to use? What data shouldn't they share? Where should they be careful?

Skills Training: They want to learn how to use these tools well and safely (remember prompt engineering from Section 4?).

Ethical Guidelines: They need to understand what's right and wrong for your business.

Learning Culture: They want to try things, sometimes fail, and share what they learn without fear.

Stop waiting for the government or big companies to give you perfect rules. They don't know your business. YOU need to lead. Start using AI thoughtfully, learn as you go, and decide what's right for YOUR situation.

HELPING YOUR TEAM SUCCEED

So how do you help your team? Start by understanding where they are now.

Think About This: Look at your team. How do they usually feel about new technology? Are they quick to try new things, nervous about change, or somewhere in between? Based on that, what kind of help will they really need to use AI well and safely?

That help doesn't have to mean expensive training programs at first. It can be:

Good Resources: Point them to quality online courses or helpful YouTube channels (yes, YouTube has amazing, up-to-date AI tutorials - often news about AI hits YouTube creators before anywhere else).

Team Workshops: Run meetings about specific tools or skills, like prompt engineering.

Expert Help: Bring in outside help (like our company) for targeted advice.

Learning Together: Encourage people already using AI to share what they've learned.

One warning: watch out for people who call themselves "AI experts." This field changes so fast that anyone claiming to know everything is probably exaggerating. Look for knowledgeable guides who focus on real business results, not gurus selling magic solutions. If someone says they're the perfect expert, feel free to tell them to get lost. Focus on practical knowledge and real-world use.

From Theory to Reality – Deploying AI Tools in Your Business

You've picked your tools (Section 2), you've prepared your team (Section 5), and now it's time for the real test: actually making AI work in your business. This is where ideas meet real life. It's exciting, but it's also where things can go wrong if you're not careful.

Let me be very clear: This section is NOT about teaching you to become a computer scientist and build AI from scratch. Forget that. That's a different job that needs special skills most businesses don't need right now.

What we're focused on here, is the practical steps for using the AI tools you've chosen - getting them working, helping people use them well, and making sure they bring real value to your business.

Look at it this way: You bought a powerful new machine for your factory (the AI tool). Now you need a plan to install it safely, train people to use it, connect it to your current work, and measure how well it's working - without causing problems or breaking something else.

It may sound similar to what we talked about with choosing tools in Section 2, and in some ways, it is. But now we're going deeper. We're moving from picking tools based on what they MIGHT do, to actually making them work for specific jobs and tasks.

The Golden Rule: Start Small, Not Big!

The biggest mistake I see businesses make at this point is trying to do everything at once. They get excited, see the potential, and want to roll out the new AI tool to everyone overnight. This "big bang" approach almost always ends badly.

Why? Because you WILL run into problems you didn't expect. The tool might be harder to connect than you thought. People might struggle to use it. The results might not be exactly what you wanted at first. You might need to change how you handle data privacy.

Trying to fix these problems for the whole company at once is like trying to fix an airplane while it's flying with everyone on board. Stressful, risky, and likely to end badly.

The smarter way? Start with a small test. Begin small, controlled, and focused.

Imagine you want to use that AI phone assistant we talked about earlier to answer your company's phones. Instead of replacing your human receptionist on day one, you'd run a small test:

- Maybe the AI answers calls after business hours at first
- Or it handles calls for just one department to start
- Or it answers only a few common questions, sending everything else to a person

This lets you test, learn, and make improvements in a safe way before expanding to more areas.

Own Your AI - Stop Renting and Start Building

Let's talk about something that costs businesses money every single month: software subscriptions. You pay for this tool, that app, this service... and the costs keep adding up. Month after month, year after year.

But what if you could OWN your AI tools instead of renting them?

The Hidden Cost of "Free" AI

When you use tools like ChatGPT, you're paying monthly fees. If you stop paying, you lose access. Your data goes through their servers. You're limited by their rules, their speed, their way of doing things.

But there's another way: **Open-source AI.**

What is Open-Source AI?

Think of it like cooking. With regular AI, you order takeout every night. It's easy, but expensive, and you can't change the recipe.

With open-source AI, you own the kitchen. You have the recipe, the ingredients, the tools. You can change things to suit your taste. You make it exactly how you want it.

Small Models, Big Results

Here's something most people don't know: You don't need a massive, expensive AI model to do specific jobs well.

Imagine you need AI to handle customer complaints for your shoe store. You could use ChatGPT (which knows everything about everything), or you could train a tiny AI model that knows ONLY about shoes and customer service.

This tiny model could:

- Run on your phone
- Work faster than ChatGPT for shoe questions

- Keep all data private on your device
- Cost nothing after setup
- Be customized exactly for your business

It's like having a specialist instead of a generalist. The specialist does one job perfectly.

Replace Your Monthly Bills

It's an unfortunate fact. We all pay bills.

Think about all the software you pay for each month:

- Email marketing tools
- Customer service chatbots
- Content generators
- Data analysis software

What if you could replace ALL of these with custom tools you actually own?

Here's the magic: AI can help build these tools for you!

You don't need to be a coding genius. You can tell AI: "Build me a customer service chatbot for my bakery that knows our products and handles common complaints." The AI writes the code. You test it. You tweak it. Soon you have a tool that works exactly how you want it.

All You Need is the Right Hardware

Here's what you need to make this happen:

1. A powerful enough computer
2. The right setup
3. A little time to learn

That's it.

Run AI Models Privately: The Foundation of Digital Sovereignty

What it means: Instead of sending prompts to a model hosted on Google's, Microsoft's, or OpenAI's servers, the entire AI process—from input to output—happens on hardware that resides within your company's physical or cloud infrastructure.

Why it's a game-changer: This is the bedrock upon which all other benefits are built. Private operation means you are not subject to the whims, terms of service, or strategic pivots of another company. A third-party provider could change their API, deprecate a model you rely on, or experience a service outage that brings your operations to a halt. With private infrastructure, you control the runtime, the model versions, and the availability. Your AI capabilities are not dependent on anyone else's uptime.

Keep Your Data Secure: The Non-Negotiable for Modern Business

What it means: Your sensitive, proprietary, and regulated data never leaves your controlled environment. It is processed entirely on your own servers, never touching a third-party data center where it could be exposed or, in some cases, used for training future public models.

Why it's a game-changer: For industries like finance, healthcare, and law, this isn't just a benefit—it's a requirement. Running AI privately is the most robust way to ensure compliance with regulations like HIPAA, GDPR, and FINRA. It protects your most valuable assets: your intellectual property, your customer data, and your strategic plans. You eliminate the risk of a data breach occurring through a third-party API and gain the ability to assure your clients and stakeholders that their information is held under the strictest, most secure protocols possible.

Build Custom Tools: Your Unfair Competitive Advantage

What it means: You are no longer limited to the generic, one-size-fits-all applications offered by public AI platforms. You can take open-source models and fine-tune them on your own unique datasets, creating bespoke AI tools that are perfectly tailored to your business's specific needs.

Why it's a game-changer: Your internal processes, customer interactions, and industry knowledge are unique. An off-the-shelf AI tool cannot understand the nuances of your company's documentation, the specific jargon of your industry, or the patterns in your proprietary data. By building custom tools, you can:

- Create an internal "expert" chatbot trained on every product manual, HR policy, and client report ever written.
- Develop a tool for your legal team that drafts initial contracts based on thousands of your past successful agreements.
- Build a customer support agent that not only answers questions but does so in your company's exact brand voice and with deep knowledge of your product history.

These are capabilities your competitors cannot simply buy or replicate.

Stop Paying Monthly Fees: The Shift from OpEx to Strategic CapEx

What it means: You transition from paying a recurring, variable operational expense (OpEx) for every API call to making a one-time capital expenditure (CapEx) on hardware. While there are still electricity and maintenance costs, the per-use cost plummets to near zero.

Why it's a game-changer: As your reliance on AI grows, so do your monthly subscription bills. These costs can be unpredictable and scale aggressively with usage, making long-term budgeting a challenge. Private infrastructure offers cost predictability and, at scale, a dramatically lower total cost of ownership. The initial investment in hardware is amortized over years of use, while the value it generates—through increased productivity and new capabilities—can be limitless. You are investing in an asset, not just renting a service.

Work Faster and Better: The Ultimate Performance Gain

What it means: By hosting models on your local network, you eliminate the latency of sending data back and forth across the internet. You also remove the usage caps and rate limits imposed by public API providers.

Why it's a game-changer: Speed is a competitive weapon. Private AI delivers near-instantaneous responses, enabling real-time applications that are impossible with cloud-based APIs. Employees can get instant feedback and assistance without waiting. You can process massive datasets—analyzing millions of customer records or thousands of documents—in a fraction of the time, without worrying about hitting an API limit that would halt your project. This translates directly to faster decision-making, quicker project turnaround, and a more agile, responsive organization.

In summary, owning your AI infrastructure transforms it from a simple utility into a core strategic asset. It's the difference between renting a generic office and building a custom headquarters designed perfectly for your company's mission. The investment provides unparalleled control over security, customization, cost, and performance, setting the foundation for a future where AI is not just a tool, but the very engine of your business.

The Real Power of Ownership

When you own your AI tools:

- You control everything
- No monthly fees after setup
- Your data stays private
- You can change anything you want
- You're not dependent on anyone else

Think about it this way: Would you rather rent your office building forever, or own it outright? Would you rather lease your delivery trucks, or own them?

Your AI tools are no different.

Getting Started

Getting started with local AI is not as hard as you think. You don't need to change everything at once. Think of it like building with Legos. You don't build the whole castle at the start. You build one small Lego piece, see how it fits, and then add another.

Start small. Pick one job you want to fix and go from there.

Step 1: Pick One Thing to Fix

You don't need to replace everything at once. Start small by picking one tool you pay for every month that you want to replace.

This is your first target. It should be something that:

- Costs a good bit of money.
- Does a pretty simple job.
- Doesn't use secret company info.

Find a team member who loves using that tool. They can be your "test pilot" and help you see if your new AI tool works as well.

Step 2: Make a Simple Test Tool

Now, build a simple AI tool to do that one job.

Don't try to make it perfect. The goal is to make a test version. A "prototype" is just a first try to see if something works.

To keep it simple:

Use a ready-made brain. Don't build an AI from scratch. Use a popular open-source model that already knows how to do the job.

Just make the main part work. Your first tool can be super basic. A box to type in and a button to get an answer. That's it!

Use assistant tools. There are free programs that help you build the outside of your app fast. Use them!

This first version is just to prove you can do it.

Step 3: Try It Out and Make It Better

Now it's time to test. Give your new test tool to your "test pilot."

Have them use your new tool and the old tool side-by-side. Ask them simple questions:

"Which one gave a better answer?"

"Was it faster or slower?"

"What's missing from the new one?"

Then, take that feedback and make it better. This is called "iterating." You just keep making small changes to fix problems and add cool stuff. Each change makes your tool a little more awesome.

Step 4: Do It Again with Something New

You did it! You built a tool that works and saves money. Now you can expand from there.

You have two choices:

1. **Fix another tool.** Pick another monthly bill and build a new AI tool to replace it. You already know how!
2. **Add more cool stuff.** Go back to your first tool and add new features. Make it faster, smarter, and more helpful.

By starting small, you learn as you go. Each small win gives you the confidence and the skills to do even bigger things with your own local AI.

The best part? Once you build one tool, you'll see how easy it is to build more. Soon you'll have a collection of custom AI tools that work exactly how you want them to, without any monthly bills.

This is what AI ownership really means: freedom, control, and keeping more money in your pocket.

Is Open-Source AI Good Enough? The Answer Might Surprise You

Let's address the question I hear most often when I talk about open-source AI: "But is it actually GOOD enough? Can it really compete with paid tools like ChatGPT?"

The answer is simple: **Yes. 100% yes.**

The Proof is in the Pudding

Here's something that should tell you everything you need to know: OpenAI - the company that makes ChatGPT - has released their OWN open-source models. Think about that for a second. The same company charging you monthly fees for their premium AI is also giving away powerful open-source models for free.

Why would they do that? Because open-source AI isn't just "good enough" - it's becoming the standard. It's ready for serious business use, right now.

Open Source vs. Paid AI: The Real Story

When people compare open-source AI to paid tools, they often think it's like comparing a homemade car to a Ferrari. But that's not the right way to look at it.

It's more like comparing a custom-built racing car to a luxury sedan. The sedan (paid AI) is comfortable, easy to use, and does everything reasonably well. The racing car (open-source AI) is built for one specific purpose and does it better than anything else.

For business tasks, this means:

- Open-source models can be fine-tuned to understand YOUR industry perfectly
- They can learn YOUR company's specific language and processes
- They can be optimized for YOUR exact use case
- They run on YOUR hardware, so no ongoing costs

Beyond AI: The Open-Source Revolution

This isn't just happening with AI. Look at automation tools, project management software, customer service platforms - all those expensive, complicated systems that cost thousands per month?

They now have open-source alternatives that you can run yourself. Instead of paying $500/month for automation software, you can run an open-source version on your own computer. Your only cost is electricity - which your business is already paying for anyway.

Let's talk about money. When it comes to AI, you have two choices: you can rent your tools, or you can buy your own. It's like renting an apartment forever or buying a house. Renting is easy at first, but the money is gone forever. Buying costs more up front, but it's yours, and it saves you a ton of cash over time.

Let's break down the math.

Choice 1: The "Renting" Way (Paid AI Tools)

This is how most people start. You pay a monthly bill for different tools. It seems simple, but the costs add up fast.

ChatGPT Plus: $20/month for each person on your team.

Specialized AI Tools: Need a tool for writing or a tool for making pictures? That's another $50-200/month for each one.

Automation Platforms: Want to connect all your tools? That can be $100-500/month.

Let's see what that looks like for a small team of 10 people:

- **Cost per employee:** $170 - $720 each month.
- **Cost for 10 employees:** $1,700 - $7,200 every single month.
- **Total cost for one year:** $20,400 - $86,400!

That's a lot of money! And the worst part? At the end of the year, you've spent all that cash, and you don't own anything. If you stop paying, all your tools disappear.

Choice 2: The "Buying" Way (Your Own AI)

This means you buy your own computer and AI brain one time. It's a bigger cost at the start, but then you own it.

One-time hardware cost: $5,000 - $50,000. (This is like buying your own super-smart computer that lives in your office.)

Monthly costs: After you buy it, what do you pay? Mostly just electricity!

Electricity cost: $20-50/month. (It's a powerful computer, so it uses a bit more power, like a fancy gaming PC.)

Let's look at the math for this way:

- **Total monthly cost:** Just $20 - $50.
- **Total cost for one year:** $240 - $600.

LET'S COMPARE THE SAVINGS

Now for the fun part. How much money do you save?

Your first-year savings: Even after buying the computer, you save $19,800 to $85,800 in your very first year!

Your second-year savings: In the second year, you save $20,160 to $85,800 because you already own the computer!

After the first year, you are saving **over $20,000 every single year.** Every year after that is almost pure profit, because your biggest cost is already paid for. You're not just paying a bill anymore; you've built a real asset for your company that makes you better, faster, and richer.

If you want to see the numbers for your own team, we have a free ROI calculator at the back of this book. It will help you figure out exactly how much you can save.

Performance That Surprises

Here's a secret most people don't know: Your own AI can be better than the big, famous paid tools.

It sounds crazy, right? How can something you build in your office be better than a tool made by a giant company?

Think of it like this: A paid AI like ChatGPT is like a very smart encyclopedia. It knows a little bit about everything in the whole world. It's amazing for general knowledge.

But a custom AI that you build is like an expert employee who has worked at your company for 10 years. This expert doesn't just know about "business"; they know *your* business. They know your customers, your products, and your inside jokes.

That's the difference. You can train your open-source AI on **YOUR** data. It learns from **YOUR** customers, **YOUR** products, and **YOUR** way of talking.

We've seen this happen over and over. We helped businesses

build open-source AI that:

Writes better marketing copy. It doesn't just write generic ads. It knows your exact customer profile—their problems, their hopes, the words they use. So it writes ads that feel like they're talking directly to a friend, not a robot.

Handles customer service like a pro. It understands your products perfectly. It knows the common questions, the tricky parts, and the simple fixes. It can give customers a real, helpful answer instead of just sending them a link to a boring help page.

Analyzes data more accurately. It's trained on your specific sales numbers and customer metrics. It knows what a "good month" looks like for you. It can spot trends and give you insights that a generic AI would completely miss because it doesn't know your business.

The surprise isn't just that you save money. The real surprise is that your own tool, built for your one specific job, can do that job better than any tool you can rent. It's not just a cheaper way to work; it's a smarter way to work.

The Win-Win-Win Situation

This is what I call the "win-win-win" situation:

Win #1: You save money - No more monthly subscriptions eating into your profits

Win #2: You get better results - Custom tools that work exactly how you need them to

Win #3: You own your assets - Building real business value instead of renting tools

Ready for Business Today

When you say open-source AI, there's an assumption that it's highly technical. The idea that open source is "for tech geeks" or "not ready for serious business". This is not the case at all. In fact, it is outdated thinking. Major companies, government agencies, and successful startups are all using open-source AI right now. Companies such as Microsoft, Meta, Google, U.S. Department of Defense and Federal Agencies all use open-source AI for their business.

The question isn't whether open-source AI is good enough. The question is why you're still paying for tools you could own.

Your Next Step

Start looking at your current monthly software expenses. Add them up. Then ask yourself: "What could I do with an extra $20,000-80,000 per year?"

That's not just savings - that's money you could invest in growing your business, hiring more people, or taking home as profit.

Open-source AI isn't coming - it's here. And businesses that embrace it now are going to have a massive advantage over those who keep paying rent on their technology.

The Future of Business is Software - Are You Ready?

Let me paint you a picture of what's coming. It's not years away - it's happening right now.

AI has become so good at coding that we can now create basically anything we can imagine without the need of a massive development team or external agency. This changes everything for small businesses. The future isn't just about using AI - it's about BECOMING a software company, even if you think you're in a completely different industry.

From Services to Software

Think about how business works today. You meet clients in person, spend hours in meetings, go back and forth on emails, negotiate deals, write contracts, discuss prices. All of this takes time - lots of it.

Now imagine this instead: Your best clients, the ones who've spent thousands with you over years, get their own custom dashboard. Or their own project management system. Or their own AI assistant that knows everything about their history with you.

This isn't science fiction. This is what AI makes possible right now.

The Personal Touch at Scale

Here's what's amazing about this shift: You can offer your VIP clients something that feels MORE personal than what you can do in person, while spending LESS time doing it.

Imagine your top client logs into their custom portal and sees:

- Their entire history with you
- Projects you're working on together
- Predictions about what they'll need next
- An AI assistant that answers questions instantly
- Automated reports tailored to their business

This isn't just better service - it's a completely different level of value. And the AI handles 80-90% of the work automatically.

Why This Changes Everything

Think about your current business model. If you're in the services industry, you probably charge by the hour, by the project, or by the month. You're limited by how many hours you can work, how many clients you can serve.

Now imagine charging for access to a software system that serves hundreds of clients automatically. Your income isn't tied to your time anymore. It's tied to the value your software creates.

This is how small businesses will scale in the AI age. Not by hiring more people, but by building better software.

The Cost Trap That's Coming

But here's the warning: If you build this future using paid AI tools, your costs will explode.

Let's say you create a custom dashboard for 100 of your best clients.

Each dashboard uses AI to:

- Analyze client data
- Generate reports
- Answer questions
- Make predictions

Using paid AI APIs (the key to use data from a system or provider that you pay for), that might cost you $5-10 per client per month. For 100 clients, that's $500-1,000 per month just in AI costs. Add in the software hosting, maintenance, and updates, and you're looking at $2,000-3,000 monthly before you even make a profit.

Now multiply that as you grow to 500 clients, then 1,000 clients. Suddenly your "scalable" business model becomes a money pit.

The Open-Source Advantage

This is where open-source AI becomes not just smart, but essential.

When you own your AI, it's like having a superpower. You're not just renting a tool; you're building a machine that is perfectly made for you. This gives you four big advantages that other businesses don't have.

1. Your Costs Don't Explode

Think about paid AI tools. The more you use them, the more you pay. If your business doubles, your AI bill doubles, too! It's like a taxi that keeps the meter running forever.

But when you own your AI, the cost is different. You buy the computer one time. After that, your main cost is just the electricity. You can have 10 customers or 10,000 customers, and your AI bill stays almost the same. This lets you grow your business without worrying that your tech costs will grow out of control.

2. You Can Make an Expert Brain

Paid AI tools are like smart generalists. They know a little about a lot of things.

But when you own your AI, you can teach it to be an expert in your job. This is called fine-tuning. It's like taking a smart person and sending them to a special school to learn everything about your industry.

If you're a lawyer, you can train your AI on thousands of your old legal documents. It will learn your specific way of writing and thinking. If you're a baker, you can train it on all your recipes. It will become the world's best AI baker. You get a tool that knows your business inside and out.

3. Your Secrets Stay Safe

This is a big one. When you use a paid AI tool, you have to send your information to their computers. Your customer lists, your secret plans, your financial numbers—it all has to leave your building.

When you own your AI, everything stays inside your office. Your data never goes anywhere. It's like keeping your diary in a locked safe in your room instead of mailing it to a stranger to read for you. For businesses that handle private information, this isn't just a nice idea; it's the only way to work.

4. You Can Change Everything

Paid tools are like a rental apartment. You can hang a few pictures, but you can't knock down a wall. You're stuck with the kitchen and bathroom they give you.

When you own your AI, you own the whole house. You can change anything you want. Don't like the way it talks? Change its personality. Need it to work with a weird old program in your office? You can build a special connection just for that. You can make it look, feel, and work exactly how you want it to. You are not just a user; you are the boss of your tool.

Instead of paying $10 per client per month, you might pay $50-100 in electricity for your entire system, whether you have 100 clients or 10,000.

Your New Business Model

Let's talk about how you make money. The old way of doing business is broken. It's based on trading your time for money. But AI gives us a new way, a better way.

The Old Way: Trading Time for Money

Most of us do business in a particular way that usually involves things like:

Meet clients in person. You drive to their office or meet them for coffee.

Spend hours on calls and meetings. Your calendar is full of back-to-back Zoom calls.

Do manual work for each client. You write every report, make every slide, and send every email by hand.

Charge by the hour or project. If you want to make more money, you have to work more hours.

Limited by your time. You can only work so many hours in a day.

There's a ceiling on how much you can earn.

The New Model: Building Value, Not Trading Hours

Thanks to AI, we have a new model. This model is about adding as much value as possible without having to strain yourself.

Build custom software for your industry. You don't just give advice; you build a tool that gives the advice for you.

AI handles 80% of the work automatically. The AI does the boring, repetitive stuff, leaving you free to do the creative, high-level work.

Clients get 24/7 access to personalized tools. Your clients don't have to wait for you to be in the office. They can get help from your AI tool anytime, day or night.

Charge monthly for software access. Instead of charging by the hour, you charge a flat fee each month for access to your amazing tool.

Limited only by your software's capabilities. You're not limited by your time anymore. You're limited by how good your software is. You can serve 10 clients or 10,000 clients, and the work doesn't get any harder for you.

Real Examples of the New Model

This isn't just a theory. People are already doing it.

A marketing consultant could build an AI dashboard. A client logs in, and the AI automatically creates ad campaigns, analyzes the results, and suggests what to do next. The consultant just checks in to make sure everything is running smoothly.

A financial advisor could create a personalized AI assistant. The AI tracks a client's investments, generates easy-to-read reports, and answers questions like "How am I doing this month?" instantly, anytime the client asks.

A business coach could build a system that analyzes a client's business. The AI looks at their sales, their website, and their marketing, then suggests improvements and tracks their progress automatically.

In this new model, you stop selling your time. You start building a valuable asset that works for you while you sleep.

Your Next Move

As I mentioned earlier, the question isn't whether this future is coming - it's already here. The question is whether you'll build it with tools you own, or tools you rent.

Every day you wait, more of your competitors are starting to build their software futures. They're creating custom dashboards, AI assistants, and automated systems that will make their services irresistible compared to old-fashioned manual work.

The businesses that thrive in the next 5 years won't be the ones with the best people skills or the biggest teams. They'll be the ones who figured out how to turn their expertise into software, tools and apps that serve thousands of clients automatically.

And the ones who build that software with open-source AI? They'll have a massive cost advantage that lets them price competitors out of the market.

The future of business is adding more value to your customers. One of the most effective ways to do this is through software, tools and apps. The only question is whether you'll own it or rent it.

SHOW ME THE MONEY! MEASURING YOUR AI OWNERSHIP ROI

We've learned why owning your AI matters, seen how open source performs just as well as paid tools, and imagined the future where every business becomes a software company. Now let's talk about the most important question: **How do we know if this is actually making us money?**

Because here's the thing - building your own AI tools and custom software feels great, but feeling great doesn't pay the bills. We need to know if our investment in AI ownership is actually boosting our bottom line.

The Two Types of AI ROI

When you own your AI instead of renting it, you get two different kinds of financial returns. One is easy to see, and the other is a total game-changer.

1. Immediate Savings (The Easy Math)

This is the simple, straightforward part. It's the money you stop spending every single month.

Monthly subscriptions you've eliminated: No more paying for ChatGPT Plus, Jasper, or Midjourney.

API costs you're no longer paying: You don't have to pay for every single question you ask the AI.

Software licenses you've replaced: That expensive data analysis tool? You can build your own.

Time saved from automation: Your team spends less time on boring tasks and more time on important work.

This is simple math: What did you used to pay per month? What do you pay now (mostly just electricity)? The difference goes straight to your profit. It's like finding money you were throwing away every month.

2. Strategic Value (The Game-Changer)

This is the part that's harder to count in dollars, but it's worth way more in the long run. Strategic value is about making your business stronger, smarter, and faster than your competition. It's the stuff that your competitors can't easily copy.

Custom tools that do exactly what your business needs. You're not stuck with a generic tool. You build a perfect tool for your one weird, specific problem that no one else has.

AI that knows your industry better than any generic tool. Your AI becomes an expert in your field. It knows your customers, your products, and your secrets. This makes your work better and your clients happier.

Software that scales without costs growing with customers. You can add 100 new customers, and your costs barely go up. Your competitors, who are renting their tools, see their bills go through the roof. You can grow faster and cheaper than anyone else.

Competitive advantages that others can't easily copy. Anyone can buy a subscription to ChatGPT. But no one else has your custom AI that you trained on your 10 years of business data. That's a moat around your business that protects you from competitors.

The immediate savings pay for the AI hardware. But the strategic value is what makes you a leader in your industry. It's the difference between saving a few bucks and building an empire.

This is harder to measure, but it's where the real money is made.

Measuring Your AI Ownership Success

Okay, so you've built your own AI. How do you know if it's actually working? You have to measure it! It's like keeping score in a game. Let's get specific about what to track.

Cost Elimination Metrics: The Money You're Saving

This is the easiest part to measure. You're looking for all the bills that have disappeared.

Total monthly subscription costs before vs. after: Add up all your AI and software bills from last year. Now add up your new, much smaller bill. The difference is your win.

Number of software tools replaced: Did you get rid of three different tools and replace them with your one custom AI? That's a huge win for simplicity and savings.

Per-employee software costs: How much did you spend on software for each person on your team before? How much do you spend now? This number should go way down.

API usage fees eliminated: If you were paying for every time your software "talked" to an AI, that bill should now be zero. That's pure profit.

Think of this like cleaning up your monthly budget. Every tool you replace and every fee you eliminate is like finding a $20 bill in your pocket every month.

Performance Metrics: How Much Better Are You?

This is about speed and quality. Is your new AI system actually making you better at your job?

How much faster does your custom AI work compared to paid tools? Time it! Does your AI write a report in 5 seconds while the old tool took 30? That's a 6x speed boost.

What percentage of tasks can your custom system automate? Look at a whole project. Can your AI do 80% of the boring work automatically? That frees up your team for the important stuff.

How many more customers can you serve with the same team? If your team used to handle 50 clients but can now handle 200 because of AI, that's a massive win. You're growing without having to hire more people.

What's the accuracy improvement on industry-specific tasks? This is a big one. Does your custom AI give you the right answer 95% of the time, while the generic tool was only right 70% of the time? That's a huge difference in quality.

Revenue Impact Metrics: The Money You're Making

This is the best part. It's not just about saving money; it's about making new money.

New revenue from custom software offerings. Are you now charging clients a monthly fee to use the cool AI tool you built? That's a brand new river of cash flowing into your business.

Increased conversion rates from personalized AI tools. Did your new AI-powered website chatbot turn more visitors into customers? If your conversion rate went from 2% to 4%, you've doubled your sales without spending more on ads.

Higher customer retention from better service. Are your customers sticking around longer because your AI gives them amazing, 24/7 support? Keeping a customer is much cheaper than finding a new one.

Premium prices you can charge for AI-enhanced services**. Can you now** charge more for your services because they're supercharged with AI? You're not just a consultant anymore; you're a high-tech consultant with a secret weapon. People will pay more for that.

The 90-Day Test

Okay, this all sounds great, but how do you prove it's working without getting overwhelmed by data? You do it with a 90-day test.

The idea is simple: you don't try to measure everything at once. That's too much work. Instead, you pick ONE area of your business to measure for 90 days. It's like a science experiment for your business. You pick one thing, watch it closely, and see what happens.

Example 1: The Customer Service Test

Let's say you want to see if your new AI customer service bot is a winner. For the next 90 days, you track just these four things:

How many customer inquiries does your custom AI handle? Is it answering 10 questions a day? 100? 500?

How much time does your team save each week? If your team used to spend 10 hours a week on simple questions and now they only spend 1, that's 9 hours of saved time.

What's the customer satisfaction score? After the AI helps a customer, ask them, "How did we do?" Is the score going up or down?

How much money did you save vs. your previous help desk software? Compare the cost of your old help desk tool to the small electricity cost of your new AI.

After 90 days, you'll have a clear story: "Our AI handled 2,000 questions, saved our team 360 hours, made customers happier, and saved us $500 a month."

Example 2: The Marketing Automation Test

Maybe you want to test your new AI marketing tool. For 90 days, you track:

How many personalized campaigns does your AI create? Is it writing 10 new ads a week for different customers?

What's the conversion rate compared to manual campaigns? Do the AI-written ads get more clicks and sales than the ones you wrote by hand?

How much time does your marketing team save? If your team used to spend a whole day writing ads and now it takes them one hour, that's a huge win.

What's the cost per lead vs. paid marketing tools? How much does it cost you to get one new customer using your AI versus using an expensive marketing tool?

After 90 days, you'll know for sure: "Our AI created 120 campaigns, doubled our conversion rate, saved our team 40 hours, and cut our cost per lead in half."

By focusing on just one area for 90 days, you get clear, powerful proof that owning your AI is one of the best business decisions you'll ever make.

The Ownership Multiplier Effect

Here's something most people miss: When you own your AI tools, the value compounds over time.

Month 1: You replace a $500/month subscription
Month 3: Your custom AI gets better at your specific tasks

Month 6: You add features that paid tools don't offer
Month 12: You have a competitive advantage that's hard to copy

Meanwhile, the person paying monthly fees is stuck with the same tool they had a year ago, but now they've paid $6,000 for it.

The Real Test: Could You Go Back?

Here's the ultimate question to ask yourself after 90 days: "If someone offered me my old setup back for free, would I take it?"

If the answer is "No way," then you know your AI ownership is delivering real value.

Beyond the Numbers

Sometimes the best return on your investment isn't something you can put in a spreadsheet. It's the feeling of being in control. It's the peace of mind that comes from knowing your business is built on solid ground.

Think about these things:

Having control over your own tools. You're not at the mercy of another company changing its rules.

Not worrying about price increases. Your costs don't suddenly double because a company decided to raise its prices.

Being able to customize anything you want. If a tool doesn't work the way you want, you can change it.

Knowing your data is private and secure. Your business secrets stay safe with you.

Building real business assets instead of renting. You're building something valuable that you own.

Disaster recovery. If the internet goes down, your AI can still work for you in your office.

No more cloud computer outages. You're not stuck waiting for a company like AWS or Cloudflare to fix a problem before you can get back to work.

These benefits don't have a price tag, but they are worth thousands of dollars in peace of mind and business stability.

Your First Measurement Dashboard

Okay, measuring all this can feel like a lot. So don't try to measure everything at once. Start with these three simple numbers.

Monthly Cost Savings: What subscriptions have you eliminated? Just add up the money you're not paying anymore.

Time Saved: How many hours per week does your team save? Ask them what tasks they don't have to do anymore.

Performance Improvement: How much better/faster/cheaper are things working? Is a task that took an hour now taking five minutes?

Track these three numbers for 30 days. If you're not seeing clear benefits in at least one area, you can adjust your approach. But if you are, and you probably will be, then it's time to expand and do even more.

The Bottom Line

Owning your AI isn't just about being tech-savvy or saving a few bucks. It's about building a business that's more profitable, more competitive, and more valuable over time.

But none of that matters if you don't measure it. Track your results, prove the value, and keep building. That's how you turn AI ownership from a cool idea into real money in your bank account.

The Future is Here - AI Meets the Real World

So far, we've talked about AI that lives on computers. But what happens when AI starts moving around in the real world? What happens when AI gets a body?

This isn't science fiction anymore. It's happening right now.

From Computer Screens to Factory Floors

Think about how automation used to work: Big, dumb machines doing the same thing over and over. A factory robot that could only weld one specific car part, or a warehouse robot that could only move boxes from point A to point B.

Now imagine something completely different:

Smart Warehouses: Picture warehouses run by teams of AI-guided robots that think for themselves. They manage inventory, pick items, pack orders, and ship everything out - all while adapting to what customers are buying in real-time. No human telling them what to do next.

Construction Sites: Imagine construction sites where autonomous machines handle the dangerous, heavy, or boring work. Digging, lifting, moving materials - all done safely and precisely by machines that can think and adapt.

Human-Robot Teams: This isn't about replacing people. It's about making people better. Picture robots working alongside your team, handling the heavy lifting, dangerous materials, or super-repetitive tasks. This frees up your people to do what humans do best: solve problems, check quality, and make smart decisions.

AI That Can Touch and Feel

Here's where it gets really exciting. For a long time, AI was just a brain in a box. It could think and write, but it couldn't do anything in the real world.

That's changing. AI is getting good at physical tasks that used to require human hands and eyes.

Think about these things:

Delivery drones that can fly over a busy city, dodge trees and power lines, and drop a package on a doorstep without a human pilot.

Specialised Robots that can perform delicate surgery, making tiny, precise cuts that a human hand might struggle to do.

AI Powered Robotic Assistants that can move like you and me, help elderly people with daily tasks, like helping them get out of a chair or fetching a glass of water.

Machines that can fix other machines. Imagine a factory where one robot breaks down, and another robot comes over, figures out what's wrong, and fixes it.

These aren't just machines following simple instructions anymore. They're AI systems that can see, feel, and make decisions in the real world. They have eyes (cameras), a brain (the AI), and hands (robotic arms). This is the next giant leap for AI, moving from just thinking to doing.

The Speed of Change is Insane

Let's talk about how fast things are moving. It's not just fast; it's crazy fast.

Think about AI-generated videos. A couple of years ago, the best we could do was make weird, blurry pictures of a cat with six legs. Today, we can create a video of Will Smith eating spaghetti that looks so real, you'd think it was filmed yesterday. We went from "kinda works" to "perfectly real" in the blink of an eye.

And it's not just videos. Think about self-driving cars. For years, they could only drive in perfect weather on empty roads. Now, they're navigating busy city streets in the rain. Think about AI writing. It went from writing like a confused robot to writing better essays than many college students.

This isn't just happening in one place. It's happening everywhere, all at once.

Your Industry Will Change

If there's one thing I want you to remember from this section, it's this: Things are changing faster than ever before.

The way your industry works today could be completely different in 3-5 years. Not just a little better—fundamentally different. Your whole business model might need to change.

If you're a lawyer, AI might soon handle most of the research and document writing, so your job will be about strategy and talking to clients, not paperwork.

If you're a graphic designer, AI might generate 100 logo ideas in 10 seconds, and your job will be about picking the best one and giving it that human touch.

If you're a doctor, AI might read thousands of X-rays and spot problems a human eye might miss, making you a super-doctor who can diagnose diseases earlier than ever before.

Don't Be the Horse and Carriage

Saying "this is how we've always done it" is like saying you'll keep using a horse and carriage because cars are "too new." It's a recipe for going out of business. The businesses that stick their head in the sand and pretend AI isn't happening will be gone. It's that simple.

Be Curious, Not Scared

This isn't about being scared. It's about being ready. The businesses that thrive will be the ones that stay curious and keep learning. They'll be the ones who say, "How can this new tool help my customers?" instead of "This new tool is scary."

The future isn't coming. It's already here. The question is, are you going to watch it happen, or are you going to be the one making it happen?

Start Thinking About This Now

This future isn't something that just happens to you, like a rainy day. You get to help shape it. But you can't shape it if you're not thinking about it. You need to start asking the right questions today, not next year.

For Your Business:

Look around your office, your factory, your store. What do you see?

What physical tasks do we do that could be automated? Think about the person who has to lift heavy boxes all day, or the worker who has to sort through a giant pile of mail.

Which jobs are dangerous, boring, or repetitive? Is someone cleaning a dangerous chemical tank? Is someone typing the same information into a computer 8 hours a day?

How could AI-powered machines make our team safer and more productive? Could a robot do the heavy lifting so that your team doesn't get hurt? Could an AI handle the boring typing so your team can focus on helping customers?

What if we could work 24/7 without getting tired? Imagine a factory that keeps making products all night long. Or a delivery service that never stops.

For Your Industry:

Now, look at your competitors. What are they doing?

How are robots and AI changing what your competitors do? Is another company in your field already using robots to build things faster and cheaper than you?

What new services could you offer with AI-powered equipment? If you're a construction company, could you use drones to inspect roofs and bridges? If you're a farmer, could you use a robot to pick fruit?

Could you build custom AI robots for your specific needs? Instead of buying a robot that's "good enough," what if you could build one that's perfect for your one weird task?

What happens when your competitors start using AI that never sleeps? They can serve customers, make products, and ship goods while you're closed for the night. How will you compete?

The Ownership Advantage

Remember what we learned about owning your AI? The same thing applies to robotics.

Instead of buying expensive, one-size-fits-all robots from big companies, imagine building custom AI-powered machines that:

Know exactly how YOUR business works. It's not a generic robot; it's your robot, trained on your processes.

Can be modified when you need something different. You can change it, upgrade it, and teach it new tricks.

Don't require monthly subscription fees. You buy it once, and it's yours.

Keep your data and processes private. Your secret way of doing things stays secret.

Work perfectly with your existing systems. It's not a clunky new tool; it's a seamless part of your team.

Small Steps, Big Impact

You don't need to transform everything overnight. This is a journey, not a race. Start small.

Look Around: What's the most physical, repetitive task in your business? That's your starting point.

Learn More: Go on YouTube and watch videos of AI robots in your industry. See what's possible.

Experiment: Try a small AI-powered tool or robot for that one task.

Measure: Does it save time? Does it save money? Does it make things safer?

Expand: If it works, do more. Find another task and repeat.

The Future is Already Here

People who say "Robots are coming" are missing the point. They're already here. Companies are using them right now to:

- Build products faster and cheaper.
- Deliver goods more efficiently.
- Keep workers safer.
- Serve customers 24/7.
- Create things that were impossible before.

The question isn't whether AI and robotics will change your business. The question is whether you'll lead that change or get left behind.

YOUR NEXT PLAY

Start paying attention to how AI and robotics are showing up in your world. Notice what's possible. Ask questions. Stay curious.

Because the businesses that succeed in the next 5 years won't be the ones with the biggest buildings or the most employees. They'll be the ones who figured out how to combine smart AI with physical machines to do things better, faster, and cheaper than anyone else.

And the ones who build and own those systems? They'll win big.

THE FOUNDATION IS SET

The theory is over. We've spent our time building the framework and adopting the right mindset for owning your AI. You understand that this book is a roadmap, not a GPS, and that you're the one in the driver's seat.

Now, it's time to put the rubber on the road.

From this point forward, we're diving into the practical, the tangible, and the immediately applicable.

These sections are pure, uncut use cases for open-source AI—real-world examples you can adapt and implement in your own business.

And there's no better place to start than the lifeblood of any company: sales and marketing.

This is where you stop guessing and start building a system that works for you 24/7.

Let's get our hands dirty.

Being Practical.

The Profitability Engine – AI for Sales and Marketing Automation

Stop Paying Rent, Start Building Equity

For years, we've treated our sales and marketing tools like a rented apartment. We pay a monthly fee for a CRM, another for an email platform, another for an ad copy generator, and another for competitor monitoring. We're paying rent on a stack of tools that we don't own and can't change. If we stop paying, our entire marketing system disappears.

The **Profitability Engine** is about flipping that model. It's where we stop paying rent and start building equity. This isn't about using

AI to write a slightly better email; it's about building an end-to-end, owned system that attracts, nurtures, and converts customers automatically. This is where you transform your sales and marketing from a collection of expensive subscriptions into a self-sustaining asset that works for you 24/7.

Let's break down how to build the three core components of your Profitability Engine.

1. Lead Scoring on Your Own Server: The Ultimate Qualifier

What it is: Lead scoring is the art of figuring out which potential customers are serious about buying and which are just browsing. The goal is to focus your sales team's time on the "hot" leads who are ready to sign a check.

Why it's important: Chasing the wrong leads is one of the biggest wastes of time and money in sales. A great lead scoring system makes your entire sales process more efficient and effective.

The Old Way: The Expensive Black Box

You pay a premium for a CRM that offers "lead scoring." It's a black box. You feed in leads, and it spits out a score based on an algorithm you can't see or control. You're paying monthly for a feature that should be yours to command.

The Owned AI Way: Your Definition of a "Hot Lead"

You build a lead scoring system that lives on your own server, using an open-source LLM. This isn't just a score; it's a reflection of your business's unique definition of a qualified lead.

How It Works: You create a pipeline that feeds incoming data directly into your model. This isn't just form fields; it's the raw text of:

- **Email Inquiries:** The initial questions, the tone, the stated urgency.
- **"Contact Us" Form Submissions:** The free-text fields where prospects describe their problems in their own words.
- **Sales Call Transcriptions:** Use a voice-to-text service and feed the transcript to your AI.

You define the criteria. You tell the model what to look for: mentions of a budget, a specific timeline, keywords related to problems you solve, and positive sentiment. The AI analyzes this unstructured data and assigns a "hotness" score from 1 to 100.

The Result: Your sales team gets a dashboard with only 80+ leads. They spend their time talking to prospects who are ready to buy, not chasing tire-kickers. You own the logic, you can tweak it anytime, and the monthly fee is zero.

2. Hyper-Personalized Ad Copy Generator: Your Brand's Voice, Amplified

What it is: This is an AI tool that writes marketing copy—like ads, emails, and social media posts—that sounds exactly like your brand.

Why it's important: Generic ad copy is invisible. Your brand's unique voice is what makes you stand out. An AI that can replicate that voice at scale is a superpower.

The Old Way: Generic or Expensive

You plug a few prompts into a generic AI like ChatGPT and get ad copy that sounds… well, like it was written by a generic AI. It's on-brand if you're lucky, and it has no memory of what made your previous campaigns successful. Or, you pay an agency a lot of money to do it for you.

The Owned AI Way: Training Your Digital Marketing Specialist

You fine-tune an open-source model exclusively on your own winning marketing materials. You're not just using an AI; you're training a digital marketing specialist that knows your business inside and out.

How It Works: You gather your secret sauce:

- All your highest-converting ad campaigns from Facebook, Google, and LinkedIn.
- Your detailed customer personas.
- Your product descriptions, value propositions, and brand voice guides.

You use this information to fine-tune a model. Now, instead of a generic prompt, you can ask it to generate five variations of a Facebook ad for "Product X" targeting "Persona Y" in the exact style of your "Summer Success" campaign.

The Result: On-brand, high-converting ad copy at the push of a button. The AI understands your nuances, your unique selling propositions, and the language that resonates with your audience. This isn't just a content generator; it's a competitive moat. You can use it for:

- **A/B Testing:** Generate 10 different ad headlines in seconds.

- **Email Campaigns:** Write a personalized email to every segment of your list.
- **Social Media:** Create a month's worth of on-brand posts in an afternoon.

3. Automated Competitor Analysis Bot: Your Free Intelligence Agency

What it is: A system that automatically watches what your competitors are doing and gives you a simple report on what's new.

Why it's important: Knowing what your competitors are up to—new products, price changes, new marketing angles—is crucial. But it's usually a huge time-sink or an expensive subscription.

The Old Way: Manual or Expensive

Competitor monitoring is either a time-consuming manual process of checking websites and social media, or an expensive subscription to a monitoring service that clutters your inbox with noise.

The Owned AI Way: Your Personal Intelligence Analyst

You build a simple, automated script that acts as your personal intelligence analyst, delivering a concise, actionable report every week.

How It Works: This is a surprisingly straightforward combination of a web scraper and an LLM.

1. **Scrape:** Use an open-source scraping tool (like Scrapy) to automatically pull text content from your top 3-5 competitors' websites, blogs, and social media profiles.

2. **Analyze:** Feed this raw text into your open-source LLM with a consistent prompt: "Analyze the following text and summarize key changes in product offerings, pricing updates, and primary marketing angles. Focus on what's new or different."

3. **Deliver:** Schedule the script to run every Monday morning and have it email the summary directly to you.

The Result: A five-minute briefing in your inbox that tells you exactly what your competitors are up to. Did they just lower their price? Are they launching a new feature? Is their new marketing campaign targeting your core customers? You'll know instantly, and you'll have paid nothing for the intel.

The 24/7 Customer Champion – Open-Source AI for Support and Success

From Cost Center to Loyalty Engine

Great marketing and sales mean nothing if your customers feel abandoned after they pay. The traditional support model is a broken game of whack-a-mole: you hire more people, buy more expensive software licenses, and still struggle to keep up. It's a cost center that drains resources.

But what if support could be a loyalty engine? What if you could build a system that makes every customer feel heard, understood, and supported 24/7, without scaling your headcount? This is where you build a customer experience so good, it becomes a competitive advantage.

Let's build systems that don't just answer questions but anticipate needs.

1. The "Knows Everything" Chatbot: Your On-Call Product Expert

What it is: A customer service chatbot that has read every single thing your company has ever written about its product. It's a true expert that can diagnose complex problems and walk users through solutions step-by-step.

Why it's important: Most chatbots are frustrating and useless. A truly knowledgeable bot can solve problems instantly, making customers feel supported and happy, while freeing up your human team for tough issues.

The Old Way: Frustrating or Expensive

You deploy a generic, frustrating FAQ bot that can only answer the three most basic questions before it says, "Let me connect you to a human." Or you pay a fortune for a "smart" chatbot platform that's a black box, charges per interaction, and still doesn't truly understand your product's nuances.

The Owned AI Way: Your Company's Brain in a Bot

You build a customer service chatbot that has read your entire collective knowledge. This is a perfect use case for a technique called **Retrieval-Augmented Generation (RAG).**

What is RAG? Think of RAG like giving an AI an open-book test. Instead of making the AI rely on its memory, you first let it search through a massive library of your information (your product docs, past support tickets, etc.). It finds the most relevant pages, and then uses that information to write a detailed, accurate answer.

How It Works:

1. **Ingest Your Knowledge:** You connect the AI to all your knowledge sources: your entire product documentation (PDFs, web pages), your internal knowledge base (Confluence, Notion), and—most importantly—the anonymized history of every past support ticket and its resolution.

2. **Answer with Context:** When a customer asks a question, the system first searches your entire knowledge base for the

most relevant information. It then feeds that information to the LLM and asks it to formulate a detailed, conversational answer based only on that context.

3. **Diagnose and Solve:** Because it has access to past ticket history, it can recognize patterns. A user describing a specific error message will get the exact troubleshooting steps that solved it for the last ten people, not just a generic link to the docs.

The Result: Instant, accurate, and deeply helpful support around the clock. Your human support team is freed from answering the same questions repeatedly and can focus on complex, high-value issues. Your customers feel like your product is incredibly intuitive and your support is magically always there.

2. Sentiment-Driven Ticket Triage: The Emotional Compass

What it is: An automated system that reads every incoming support ticket, understands the urgency and emotion behind it, and routes it instantly to the right place.

Why it's important: An angry customer who waits for 24 hours for a reply is a customer who will probably leave. Getting the right people on the right problems immediately is the key to saving relationships.

The Old Way: Slow and Subjective

A support manager spends the first hour of their day reading through every new ticket, manually assigning priority, and trying to spot the fires. It's slow, subjective, and a single angry customer can get lost in the shuffle for hours.

The Owned AI Way: Your Emotional Radar

You build an automated triage system that reads every incoming ticket and instantly points you to the customers who need help most.

How It Works: You use an open-source Natural Language Processing (NLP) model as the first line of defense for your support inbox.

1. **Analyze Incoming Traffic:** Every new support ticket, email, or chat message is automatically passed through the AI model.

2. **Tag with Urgency and Emotion:** You train or prompt the model to look for specific signals. It automatically tags tickets with labels like "Urgent: System Down," "Frustrated: Billing Issue," or "Low Priority: General Question." It can detect anger, confusion, or even

delight.

3. **Route and Alert:** Based on these tags, your system takes action. "Urgent" tickets are automatically moved to the top of the queue. If the AI detects a spike in negative sentiment around a specific feature (e.g., five "Frustrated" tickets about the new dashboard in one hour), it can automatically send a Slack alert to the product and support managers.

The Result: The most critical, at-risk customers get an immediate response, dramatically reducing the chance of them churning. Your team can focus their energy where it's needed most. Management gets real-time insights into product problems and customer sentiment, allowing them to be proactive instead of reactive.

3. Proactive Customer Health Monitoring: Nipping Churn in the Bud

What it is: A system that monitors your customers' product usage and identifies signs of trouble before the customer even realizes there's a problem.

Why it's important: The best customer support is the kind you never have to use. By solving problems before they become big, you turn potential failures into moments of delight and build incredible loyalty.

The Old Way: Reactive and Too Late

Customer success is reactive. You wait for a customer to stop using the product, complain, or—worst case—submit a cancellation notice. By the time you reach out, the damage is often already done.

The Owned AI Way: Your Crystal Ball for Customer Happiness

You build a system that monitors your customers' product usage and identifies signs of trouble before the customer even realizes there's a problem.

How It Works: This connects the power of AI directly to your application's data.

1. **Connect to Usage Data:** Using an API, you give your AI read-only access to key user activity data from your app's database or analytics tool.

2. **Identify At-Risk Patterns:** You define what an "unhealthy" customer looks like. The AI runs automated checks daily for patterns like a user that hasn't logged in for 14 days, or a user who used a key feature daily has suddenly stopped, or a user repeatedly fails to complete

a crucial onboarding step.

3. **Trigger Personalized Outreach:** When the AI flags an at-risk customer, it triggers an automated, personalized action. This could be an email that says, "Hey [Name], we noticed you haven't used [Feature] lately. Here's a 2-minute video on how it can help you [achieve goal]." For high-value customers, it can automatically create a task for a human success manager to give them a call.

The Result: You dramatically reduce churn by solving problems proactively. Customers feel genuinely cared for and supported, not just like another number. Your human success team can focus on building relationships and driving expansion, not just firefighting.

The Efficiency Architect – AI for Operations and Workflow

The Back Office Revolution

Welcome to the back office revolution. This is where we tackle the invisible anchors that drag down your business: the soul-crushing, repetitive tasks that create bottlenecks, invite human error, and drain your team's energy. These are the jobs everyone hates but that have to get done.

Most companies solve this by buying more software—another subscription for expense reports, another for meeting notes, another for contract management. You end up with a tangled mess of tools that don't talk to each other and a monthly bill that keeps growing.

We're going to do the opposite. We're going to build our own efficient machines. These are smooth, automated processes that you own, that work exactly the way you work, and that cost nothing to run.

Let's design a better way to operate.

1. Intelligent Invoice and Receipt Processor: The End of Data Entry

What it is: A system that automatically "reads" your invoices and receipts, pulls out the important information, and puts it into your accounting software for you.

Why it's important: Manual data entry is the definition of tedious work. It's boring, prone to errors, and a terrible use of a smart person's time. Automating it frees up your team for more valuable work.

The Old Way: Manual or Expensive

You or your team member spends hours every month hunched over a stack of receipts, manually typing vendor names, dates, and amounts into your accounting software. Or you pay a hefty monthly fee for a service like Dext or Expensify, which is essentially just renting a black box that does the same thing.

The Owned AI Way: Your Own Data Entry Robot

You build your own processing system that lives on your server. It uses computer vision to "read" your invoices and receipts, extracts the exact data you need, and posts it directly into your accounting software, ready for your approval. It's fast, it's accurate, and it's 100% yours.

How It Works: This is a classic and surprisingly achievable AI project.

1. **Scan and Extract:** You set up an email address (e.g., receipts@yourcompany.com) where you forward all PDF invoices and photos of receipts. An automated script checks the inbox, and for each new attachment, it uses an open-source computer vision model to analyze the image or PDF.

2. **Parse the Data:** The raw text is then fed into a small, fine-tuned language model that has been trained to understand invoice layouts. It identifies and extracts the key fields: Vendor Name, Invoice Number, Date, Total Amount, and line-item details.

3. **Post to Accounting:** The script then uses the API for your accounting software (like Xero or QuickBooks) to create a new draft bill or expense, populating all the fields with the extracted data.

The Result: The soul-crushing task of manual data entry is eliminated. Your bookkeeper or accountant now spends their time on high-value analysis, not tedious typing. You save hundreds or thousands of dollars a year on subscription fees and have a system that is perfectly tailored to your business's specific invoice formats.

2. The "Smart Meeting Assistant": From Talk to Action

What it is: A bot that joins your virtual meetings, transcribes everything, and automatically pulls out the action items and assigns them to the right people in your project management tool.

Why it's important: How many times have you left a meeting and no one was quite sure who was supposed to do what? This system creates perfect accountability and frees everyone to actually participate in the meeting instead of just taking notes.

The Old Way: Incomplete and Manual

Someone in a meeting is designated as the note-taker, which means they're only half-participating. The notes are often incomplete, action items are vague, and after the meeting, someone has to manually type them up and then enter each task into a project management tool, hoping they assigned it to the right person.

The Owned AI Way: Your Flawless Meeting Secretary

You create a bot that joins your virtual meetings (with everyone's consent, of course). It transcribes the conversation in real-time, identifies the key decisions and action items, and automatically pushes those tasks into your project management system.

How It Works: This combines a few different AI capabilities into one powerful workflow.

1. **Join and Transcribe:** The assistant joins your Zoom or Google Meet call. The audio stream is sent to an open-source speech-to-text model (like Whisper) for real-time transcription.

2. **Summarize and Identify:** After the meeting, the full transcript is fed to an open-source LLM with a specific

prompt: "Read this transcript and identify all key decisions made. Then, list all action items, including who is responsible for each and what the task is."

3. **Integrate and Assign:** The script parses the LLM's output. For each action item, it uses the API for your project management tool (like Trello, Asana, or Jira) to create a new card/task. It uses the names identified in the transcript to assign the task to the correct team members.

The Result: Perfect meeting notes, every time. No more ambiguity about who was supposed to do what. Your project management tool is always up-to-date, creating a flawless record of accountability. Your team is freed to fully engage in meetings, knowing the administrative busywork is handled.

3. Automated Contract Analysis: Your First-Line Legal Review

What it is: An AI system that reads new contracts and instantly flags any clauses that are unusual, risky, or different from your company's standard agreements.

Why it's important: Getting a lawyer to review every contract is slow and expensive. This AI acts as a first-pass filter, so your lawyer only has to look at the important parts, saving you time and a lot of money.

The Old Way: Slow, Expensive, and Opaque

A new contract comes in from a client or vendor. It gets forwarded to your lawyer, who charges you $400 an hour to spend two hours reading it line-by-line to flag anything that deviates from your standard terms. It's a slow, expensive, and opaque process.

The Owned AI Way: Your Instant Legal Risk Detector

You train an AI model on your own company's standard contract templates and legal "playbook." When a new contract arrives, the AI performs an instant first-pass review, comparing it against your standards and flagging any unusual, risky, or non-standard clauses for human review.

How It Works: This is a perfect application for RAG (Retrieval-Augmented Generation).

1. **Build Your Knowledge Base:** You create a database of your "golden" contracts: your standard MSA, SOW, supplier agreements, etc. You also create a "risk

playbook" that outlines clauses you always reject, always modify, or require special approval for.

2. **Compare and Contrast:** When a new contract is uploaded, the AI first retrieves the most relevant sections from your standard contracts and risk playbook. It then analyzes the new document, specifically looking for deviations from your established norms.

3. **Flag and Summarize:** The AI generates a summary report. It won't give legal advice, but it will say things like: "Clause 3.2 on Liability is non-standard and differs from your template. It removes the liability cap. Flag for review." or "This contract lacks an Indemnification clause, which is present in your standard template."

The Result: A two-hour legal review is now a 10-minute check. Your lawyer can focus their expensive time only on the flagged issues, not on re-reading the boilerplate. You can review contracts in minutes, not days, dramatically speeding up your sales and procurement cycles while still protecting your interests.

Unlocking the Data Vault - Custom AI for Business Intelligence

Your Business's Gold Mine

Your business is sitting on a gold mine. Every sale, every website click, every customer support ticket, every product return is a nugget of data. Hidden in that data are the answers to your biggest questions: What are my customers really buying? Why are people leaving my website? What's the next product I should build?

But for most businesses, this gold mine is locked in a vault. The key is held by expensive BI platforms, complex SQL queries, and overworked data analysts who are buried in the backlog. You're told you need a six-figure software license and a team of specialists to "unlock" your own data. It's a lie.

The truth is, with open-source AI, you can build your own master key. You can create systems that mine your data for strategic insights on demand, turning raw numbers into the answers you need to make smarter decisions, faster.

Let's crack open the vault.

1. The Plain English Data Analyst: Insights for Everyone

What it is: A system that lets anyone on your team ask complex questions about your business data in plain English and get an instant answer, complete with a chart.

Why it's important: Right now, getting answers from your data is slow and requires a specialist. This puts a huge bottleneck between your questions and your decisions. Making data accessible to everyone makes your entire company smarter and faster.

The Old Way: Waiting and Wading

You have a question about your business. You email the data analyst and wait three days for a report. Or you try to use a complex BI tool like Tableau or Power BI, only to find yourself lost in a sea of menus and drag-and-drop interfaces, still needing to understand the underlying data structure. Getting an answer requires specialized knowledge and a lot of patience.

The Owned AI Way: Your On-Call Data Expert

You connect an open-source LLM directly to your business databases (with secure, read-only access). Now, anyone on your leadership team can ask complex questions in plain English and get an instant answer.

How It Works: This is one of the most powerful and accessible applications of LLMs.

1. **Connect and Instruct:** You give the AI secure access to your databases (e.g., your SQL database for sales, your inventory management system, your Google Analytics data). You also provide it with the database schema—a map of all the tables and columns.

2. **Translate and Query:** When you ask a question like, "What were our top 5 most profitable products last quarter for customers in the Pacific Northwest?", the AI's first job is to translate that natural language question into a perfect SQL query.

3. **Execute and Visualize:** The AI runs that query against your database. It takes the raw data it gets back and uses a simple code library to generate a clean, easy-to-read chart (like a bar chart) and a natural language summary: "The top 5 most profitable products were X, Y, and Z, accounting for 40% of total revenue in the region."

The Result: You democratize data. The CEO, the head of marketing, and the product manager can all get the answers they need instantly, without waiting for a specialist. You make faster, more informed decisions because the data is no longer locked behind a technical gatekeeper.

2. Automated KPI Anomaly Detection: The "Why" Behind the "What"

What it is: A system that not only alerts you when something important in your business goes wrong (like website traffic dropping), but also automatically investigates and tells you why it happened.

Why it's important: Knowing what happened is only half the battle. The real value is in knowing why. This system turns your team from reactive firefighters into proactive problem-solvers.

THE OLD WAY: VAGUE ALERTS AND GUESSING

You set up simple alerts in your analytics software. "Alert me if website traffic drops by 20%." The alert fires, and you get a notification that says, "Website traffic dropped by 20%." You know what happened, but you have no idea why. Now begins the manual, frustrating detective work: "Did we break the site? Did our ads stop running? Did a competitor do something?"

THE OWNED AI WAY: YOUR DIGITAL DETECTIVE

You build a system that not only detects the anomaly but also acts like a digital detective, automatically analyzing other event streams to suggest a likely cause. It gives you the "why" along with the "what."

How It Works: This system connects your KPI data to your business's event logs.

1. **Monitor and Detect:** The AI constantly monitors your key metrics (e.g., website traffic, conversion rate, cart abandonment). It uses a statistical model to detect when a metric behaves abnormally compared to its historical pattern.

2. **Cross-Reference Events:** The moment an anomaly is detected, the AI triggers an investigation. It queries other systems for events that happened at the exact same time: your deployment logs (Did we just push a new version of the code?), your marketing automation platform (Did a big ad campaign end?), your server error logs (Is there a spike in 500 errors?).

3. **Hypothesize and Alert:** The AI uses an LLM to correlate the anomaly with these events and generates a smart alert. Instead of "Traffic dropped 30%," you get: "Traffic dropped 30% at 2:05 PM. This coincides with the deployment of version 2.1. Recommend immediate rollback."

The Result: You slash your mean-time-to-resolution (MTTR) for critical issues. You move from reactive firefighting to proactive diagnosis. Your team spends less time guessing and more time fixing the root cause.

3. Customer Feedback Synthesizer: The Voice of the Customer, Quantified

What it is: An AI-powered system that pulls in customer feedback from every source—surveys, reviews, support tickets—and automatically groups it into key themes, telling you what your customers are really saying.

Why it's important: Customer feedback is a flood of words. It's impossible to read it all, and it's easy to be swayed by the one angry person who yelled the loudest. This system turns that messy flood into a clean, data-driven report.

The Old Way: Overwhelming and Subjective

Customer feedback is scattered everywhere: surveys, app store reviews, support tickets, social media mentions. Trying to make sense of it all means reading hundreds or thousands of individual comments. It's overwhelming, time-consuming, and easy to miss the quieter, more widespread issues.

The Owned AI Way: Your Unbiased Customer Expert

You build an AI-powered funnel that ingests feedback from every source, automatically groups it into key themes, and gives you a weekly, data-driven summary of what your customers are really saying.

How It Works: This is a job for an LLM's pattern-recognition and summarization capabilities.

1. **Ingest Everything:** You use APIs to pull in raw text from all your feedback channels: your survey tool (e.g., SurveyMonkey), the app stores (Apple/Google Play), and your helpdesk software (e.g., Zendesk).

2. **Cluster and Theme:** You feed this massive amount of unstructured text to an open-source LLM with a clear instruction: "Read all this feedback and identify the main topics of discussion. Group similar comments together and give each group a thematic name."

3. **Summarize and Quantify:** The AI analyzes the text and identifies recurring themes like "UI Confusion," "Feature Request: Dark Mode," "Pricing Complaints," or "Bug with Export Function." It then counts how many comments fall into each theme and generates a concise weekly report: "This week, 35% of negative feedback mentioned confusion around the new dashboard. 20% of all feedback was a request for a dark mode."

The Result: You have a clear, unbiased, quantitative view of customer sentiment. You can prioritize your product roadmap with confidence, knowing you're addressing the most common and impactful issues. You turn a subjective, messy flood of words into a clean, actionable dashboard.

The Content Engine – Scaling Your Voice with AI

From Sputtering to High-Performance

Content is the engine of modern marketing, but for most businesses, it's a sputtering, unreliable one. It's a constant battle to produce enough of it, to maintain a consistent voice across a dozen channels, and to do it all without a massive team or budget. Generic AI tools promise a solution, but they often produce bland, soulless content that sounds like every other company using the same prompts.

This section goes beyond "writing blog posts." It's about building a complete, brand-aligned content production system that can operate at scale. This is how you stop renting content creation and start owning your voice, ensuring a consistent and strategic message across everything you do.

Let's build an engine that doesn't just produce words but produces results.

1. Brand Voice Guardian: Your "Brand-in-a-Box"

What it is: An AI model that has been trained exclusively on your best content, ensuring that everything it generates—from a tweet to a technical white paper—sounds exactly like your brand.

Why it's important: A consistent brand voice builds trust. When your website, emails, and social media all sound like they came from the same personality, your brand feels more professional and reliable. This system makes that consistency automatic.

The Old Way: Dusty Guides and Endless Editing

You create a detailed brand style guide that collects digital dust. You hire freelance writers and spend hours editing their work to "sound like us." Or you use a generic AI tool and spend more time trying to engineer the perfect prompt and editing the mediocre output than it would have taken to just write it yourself.

The Owned AI Way: Your Brand's Living Soul

You create a fine-tuned open-source model that is the living embodiment of your brand. It has been trained exclusively on your most successful and on-brand content, ensuring that everything it generates is guaranteed to sound like it came directly from your company's core.

How It Works: This is where you turn your brand's unique identity into a tangible, reusable asset.

1. **Curate Your "Golden Corpus":** Gather all the content that perfectly represents your brand: your mission statement, your website's "About" page, your top-performing ad copy, your best blog posts, and your most engaging social media updates.

2. **Fine-Tune the Model:** Use this curated data to fine-tune an open-source LLM. This process goes beyond simple prompting; it adjusts the model's underlying weights to internalize your specific vocabulary, your tone (e.g., witty, professional, empathetic), your sentence structure, and your core messaging.

3. **Deploy as a Private API:** You host this fine-tuned model on your own server and expose it through an API. Now, when your marketing team needs to generate a copy, they don't go to ChatGPT—they query your model.

The Result: A perfectly consistent brand voice at scale. You dramatically reduce editing cycles and empower anyone on your team to create on-brand content. It's your brand's unique personality, captured in code and ready to be deployed anywhere.

2. Automated Content Repurposing Pipeline: Multiply Your Efforts

What it is: A "set it and forget it" workflow that takes one piece of core content (like a webinar or blog post) and automatically turns it into a dozen ready-to-publish pieces for every other channel.

Why it's important: Creating great content is hard work. This system lets you get the maximum value out of every single thing you create, saving you hundreds of hours and ensuring you have a steady stream of content for all your platforms.

THE OLD WAY: MANUAL AND DILUTED

You spend weeks producing a single, high-value piece of content, like a webinar or a detailed blog post. Then, the daunting task of repurposing it begins. Someone manually has to watch the whole thing, pull out key quotes, and try to rewrite it into different formats for different channels. It's tedious, inefficient, and the core message often gets diluted.

The Owned AI Way: The Ultimate Content Multiplication Machine

You build a workflow where your core, long-form content is automatically fed into an AI pipeline that atomizes it into a dozen ready-to-publish pieces for every channel, all while preserving the strategic message.

How It Works:

1. **Ingest Core Content:** The pipeline triggers when you upload a video file (webinar), an audio file (podcast), or a long-form text document (blog post).

2. **Transcribe and Analyze:** An open-source model like Whisper transcribes the audio/video into text. An LLM then analyzes this transcript to identify the key themes, the most surprising insights, the primary takeaways, and the most quotable soundbites.

3. **Generate and Format:** The LLM then executes a series of

pre-defined prompts based on this analysis, automatically generating:

a. A Twitter thread based on the key takeaways.
b. A professional LinkedIn post summarizing the main topic.
c. Three variations of a promotional email for your newsletter.
d. The script for a 60-second TikTok or Reels video.
e. Five pull-quotes for social media graphics.

The Result: One hour of content creation now fuels your entire content calendar for a week. Your team is freed from the manual grind of repurposing to focus on high-level strategy and creating the next core asset. You maintain a powerful, consistent presence across all platforms without manual labor.

3. SEO-Optimized Outline Generator: Your Strategic Roadmap to Ranking

What it is: A tool that acts as your personal SEO strategist. It takes a target keyword, analyzes the top-ranking competition in seconds, and generates a comprehensive, data-driven blog post outline designed to outperform them.

Why it's important: Writing a great article that nobody can find is a waste of time. This system ensures that every piece of content you create is built on a strategic foundation, dramatically increasing your chances of ranking on Google and driving organic traffic.

The Old Way: Manual Guesswork

You want to rank for a keyword, so you open a dozen browser tabs. You manually analyze the top 5 articles on Google, trying to reverse-engineer their structure, their headings, and the questions they answer. It's a time-consuming, manual process that's easy to get wrong, leading you to write an article that's destined to live on page three.

The Owned AI Way: Turning SEO into a Science

You build a tool that takes the guesswork out of SEO and gives you a clear, data-driven roadmap for your content.

How It Works:

1. **Scrape the SERP:** You give the tool a target keyword (e.g., "open-source CRM for small business"). A web scraping script automatically pulls the text content from the top 5-10 URLs on the search results page.

2. **Analyze and Deconstruct:** The AI analyzes this

collection of content. It identifies the common subheadings (H2s, H3s), the key concepts they all cover, the questions they answer (often pulled from "People Also Ask" boxes), and their average length and structure.

3. **Generate a Superior Outline:** The AI synthesizes this intelligence into a logical, comprehensive outline for your article. It will recommend H2 and H3 headings that cover all the critical ground, suggest specific topics to cover under each heading, and even recommend internal links to your own existing content to strengthen the article's authority.

The Result: You stop guessing and start writing with a strategic advantage. Your content is built on a foundation of what's already proven to rank, allowing you to focus on creating better, more comprehensive content than the competition. This dramatically increases your chances of hitting page one, turning your content from a cost center into a powerful, automated lead-generation machine.

Building Your Internal Brain – The AI-Powered Knowledge Base

The End of Knowledge Decay

Every company has a brain. But for most, it's a mess. The knowledge is scattered across a thousand Slack threads, buried in a Google Drive folder structure that no one understands, and locked away in the personal inboxes of key employees. When someone leaves, a piece of the company's brain dies with them.

The traditional solution is to buy yet another piece of software—a "knowledge base" platform—and then assign the thankless, manual task of documenting everything to an already overworked team. It's a chore everyone hates, so it never gets done right.

We're going to stop this knowledge decay. We're going to build a true internal brain—a single, queryable source of truth that captures, organizes, and retrieves your company's collective intelligence on demand. This is how you make your company smarter, faster, and more resilient.

1. The Ultimate Company "Search Bar": Finding the Needle in the Haystack

What it is: A single search bar that lets any employee ask a question and get an instant, precise answer from any of your company's internal documents—Slack, Google Drive, Confluence, and more.

Why it's important: How much time does your team waste looking for information? This system gives them that time back. It eliminates the "who do I ask?" bottleneck and makes your entire company's collective knowledge instantly accessible.

The Old Way: The Digital Wild Goose Chase

You need to find the final decision on the Q3 marketing budget. You search Google Drive and find five different versions of the budget spreadsheet. You search Slack and get 50 unrelated messages. You give up and ask your manager, who also can't remember and has to spend 20 minutes digging through their own files. The friction is immense, and the answer is often lost.

The Owned AI Way: Your Company's Answer Engine

You index every single internal document into a vector database that you host. An open-source LLM acts as the search interface, allowing any employee to ask a natural language question and get an instant, precise answer with a direct link to the source.

How It Works: This is the magic of semantic search, powered by AI.

1. **Index Everything:** You run a script that connects to all your internal tools via API. It pulls in all the text content and uses an open-source embedding model to convert it into numerical representations (vectors) that capture the meaning of the text. These vectors are stored in a vector database you control.

2. **Query with Meaning:** When an employee asks, "What was the final decision on the Q3 marketing budget?", the LLM converts their question into a vector. It then searches the vector database for the pieces of text that are most semantically similar to the question.

3. **Answer and Cite:** The LLM takes the most relevant text snippets (e.g., the key messages from a Slack thread where the decision was finalized) and uses them to generate a concise, natural language answer. Crucially, it also provides direct links back to the exact Slack conversation or Google Doc where it found the information.

The Result: Your company's entire institutional knowledge is instantly accessible. You eliminate the "who do I ask?" bottleneck. Employees can find the information they need to do their jobs in seconds, not hours, dramatically increasing productivity and reducing duplicated effort.

2. Smart Employee Onboarding Assistant: The 24/7 Welcome Wagon

What it is: A specialized chatbot that acts as a dedicated onboarding assistant for every new employee. It's trained on your HR handbook, IT policies, and common questions, providing instant, accurate answers and guiding new hires through their first-week checklist.

Why it's important: A new hire's first week is critical. A smooth, consistent experience gets them productive faster and makes them feel welcome. This system automates the repetitive parts of onboarding so your team can focus on the human parts.

The Old Way: Overwhelming Managers and New Hires

A new hire's first week is a blur of meetings and questions. They rely on their manager or a designated "buddy" for everything, from "How do I set up my expense account?" to "What's our policy on remote work?" This pulls senior employees away from their work and creates an inconsistent, often overwhelming, experience for the new hire.

The Owned AI Way: Your 24/7 HR Helper

You create a specialized chatbot that acts as a dedicated onboarding assistant for every new employee.

How It Works: This is a focused, high-impact application of a chatbot.

1. Train on Company Knowledge: You feed the AI all your essential onboarding documents: the employee handbook, IT setup guides, benefits information, and company history. You can also "prime" it with the top 50 questions new hires typically ask.

2. Provide a Safe Space: The chatbot is integrated into your company's Slack or Teams. New hires can ask it anything without feeling like they're bothering someone or asking a "stupid question."

3. Guide and Automate: The AI can be proactive. On the new hire's first day, it can message them with a checklist: "Welcome! Let's get you started. Step 1: Click here to set up your payroll. Step 2: Here's the link to book your IT equipment."

The Result: A faster, more consistent, and less stressful onboarding experience. New hires become productive more quickly. HR and managers reclaim countless hours previously spent answering repetitive questions, allowing them to focus on the human elements of welcoming a new team member.

3. Automated Process Documentation: Capturing the "How"

What it is: An AI "shadow" that observes an expert performing a task and automatically generates a clear, step-by-step guide or training video script. It turns tribal knowledge into a permanent, shareable company asset.

Why it's important: So much of how a business actually runs is "tribal knowledge"—the unwritten rules and processes that live in one person's head. When that person leaves, the process leaves with them. This system captures that knowledge before it's too late.

The Old Way: Too Busy to Document

You need to document how to perform a routine but complex task, like closing the monthly books or processing a refund. The person who knows how to do it is too busy to write it down. If they do, the document is a wall of text that's hard to follow. When they leave the company, the process leaves with them.

The Owned AI Way: Your Process Photographer

You build an AI "shadow" that observes an expert performing a task and automatically generates a clear, step-by-step guide or training video script.

How It Works: This uses AI to capture the process, not just the outcome.

1. **Observe with Consent:** An employee who is the expert at a task runs a lightweight, secure recording application on their computer (with their full knowledge and

consent).

2. **Capture and Analyze:** The AI observes the user's screen activity: the applications they open, the buttons they click, the text they type, and the data they enter. It uses computer vision and sequence analysis to understand the logical flow of the process.

3. **Generate the Guide:** After the session, the AI compiles its observations into a structured document. It can generate a simple text-based SOP ("1. Open the accounting software. 2. Navigate to the 'Reports' tab...") or even a script for a training video, complete with descriptions of what's happening on screen and what the user should say.

The Result: Documentation that actually gets created and is easy to understand. You capture the nuanced, unwritten rules that experts follow. This makes training new employees faster, ensures consistency in how tasks are performed, and builds a resilient knowledge base that isn't dependent on any single individual.

Beyond the Screen – Open-Source AI for Physical Operations

Bringing AI into the Real World

So far, we've focused on the digital side of your business—the data, the documents, the customer interactions. But for many of us, the business isn't just on a screen; it's in a warehouse, on a production line, or in a physical workshop.

These physical operations are often the last place we think to apply technology. People say it's "too complex" or "too expensive." But that's not true.

You don't need a million-dollar budget or a team of robotics engineers. You need a Raspberry Pi (a cheap, small computer), a camera, and the willingness to build a system that works for you.

Let's bring AI into the real world.

1. The AI Inventory Counter: The End of Manual Stocktakes

What it is: A camera system that automatically counts your products every day, giving you perfect inventory numbers without anyone having to do manual counts.

Why it's important: Manual inventory counts are a pain. They're boring, take forever, and people make mistakes. This system does the work for you, perfectly, every single day.

The Old Way: Boring and Error-Prone

You or your team spend the last Saturday of the month walking the warehouse with a clipboard, manually counting boxes. It's tedious, it's disruptive, and it's prone to human error. Or, you invest in an expensive, proprietary inventory system with specialized scanners and complex software that locks you into their ecosystem.

The Owned AI Way: Your 24/7 Inventory Assistant

You set up a simple, automated camera system that counts your stock for you every single day, without anyone lifting a finger.

How It Works: This is simpler than you think.

1. **The Hardware Setup:** All you need is a Raspberry Pi (a $75 computer the size of a credit card), a good quality camera module, and a power supply. You mount this setup in a fixed position overlooking a key section of your warehouse or storeroom shelves.

2. **The AI Model:** You use an open-source computer vision model, like Qwen3 VL, which is excellent at detecting objects in images. You train this model on a few dozen photos of your products or packaging, teaching it to recognize "Product A," "Product B," and so on.

3. **The Automated Workflow:** You write a simple script that tells the camera to take a photo at the same time every day (e.g., 6 PM, after the warehouse is closed). The script runs the image through your trained AI model, which counts the number of each product it sees. It then uses an API to automatically update the stock levels in your inventory management system.

The Result: Perfect, daily inventory visibility without the labor cost and pain of manual counts. You can set up automatic alerts for when stock is low, preventing stockouts before they happen. You reduce shrinkage from misplaced or stolen items because you know exactly what should be on the shelf.

2. Quality Control Inspector: The Tireless Eye for Perfection

What it is: An AI system that looks at every product coming off your production line and spots defects that humans might miss.

Why it's important: Human inspectors get tired. Their eyes hurt. They miss things, especially at the end of a long day. An AI never gets tired and never has a bad day.

The Old Way: Tired Human Eyes

You pay a human employee to stand at the end of a production line and inspect every single item. It's monotonous work. Their eyes get tired, their attention wanes, and inevitably, a defective product slips through. Their consistency varies from morning to afternoon, and from person to person.

The Owned AI Way: Your Perfect Inspector

You build an AI-powered inspector that works 24/7/365 with the same level of focus and consistency.

How It Works:

1. **The Setup:** You install a stationary camera and good lighting over a specific point on your production line, where every product passes by.

2. **Training the Model:** You create a "training set" of images: hundreds of photos of your "perfect" product, and hundreds of photos of every type of defect you want to catch (e.g., scratches, dents, misaligned labels, incorrect color). You use these images to train a classification model to distinguish between "good" and "bad."

3. **Real-Time Inspection:** As each product comes down the line, the camera captures an image and feeds it to the AI model in real-time. If the model classifies the product as "defective," it can trigger an immediate physical alert (like a flashing light or a buzzer) to pull the item off the line.

The Result: A massive leap in quality consistency. You dramatically reduce the number of defective products that reach your customers, protecting your brand reputation. You free up your human employees from a mind-numbing task and reassign them to more valuable work, like process improvement.

3. Smart Security and Access: Your Private, On-Site Security Guard

What it is: A system that uses facial recognition to control who can enter your building, running entirely on your own hardware.

Why it's important: Physical keys get lost. Keycards get shared. Monthly security services are expensive and own your data. This system gives you better security for less money, and you own all the data.

The Old Way: Lost Keys and Monthly Fees

You manage keys and keycards, which are constantly lost and need to be replaced. Or you pay a monthly subscription to a third-party security service that manages your access control, holds your data (including video feeds and access logs) on their servers, and can raise prices at any time.

The Owned AI Way: Your Personal Security Expert

You build your own intelligent access control system using open-source facial recognition that runs entirely on your own hardware.

How It Works:

1. **Local Hardware:** You install a small, powerful computer (like a Raspberry Pi or a mini-PC) and a camera at each entry point. This is the "brain" of the system, and it lives on-site, connected to your network, not the cloud.

2. **Privacy-First Recognition:** You use an open-source facial recognition model. During a one-time setup, each authorized employee has a few photos taken to create a secure, mathematical representation of their face (this data is stored locally on your machine, never sent to the cloud). When someone approaches the door, the camera captures their face, the model compares it to the stored representations, and if there's a match, it triggers a smart lock to open the door.

3. **Intelligent Logging and Alerts:** The system logs every entry and exit with a timestamp and a snapshot, all stored locally. If the camera detects a face that isn't in the database of authorized employees, it can deny access

and instantly send a security alert to your phone or a manager's Slack channel.

The Result: A seamless, keyless entry experience for your employees. You eliminate the recurring costs of a third-party service and the hassle of managing physical keys. Most importantly, you have complete data privacy and sovereignty—your building's security data belongs to you, and you alone.

The Ethical Owner – Responsible AI in Your Business

Owning the Consequences

We've covered how to build AI systems that save you money, make you more money, and free up your time. But there's one final, critical piece of the puzzle. Building an owned AI system isn't just about controlling the technology; it's about owning the consequences.

Too often, ethics are treated as an afterthought—a box to check for the legal department or a PR statement to put on a website. That's a mistake. Building trust with your customers and your employees isn't a "soft" skill; it's a long-term competitive advantage.

A business that is known for being fair, private, and reliable will win every time.

This section isn't a preachy lecture on morality. It's a practical, no-nonsense guide to building AI that you can be proud of, and that protects your business from the costly mistakes that come from cutting corners.

1. Building a "Privacy by Design" Checklist

What it is: A simple checklist you run through before building any new AI tool to make sure you're protecting your customers' data from day one.

Why it's important: Privacy isn't just about following laws (though that's important). It's about respecting your customers. When they trust you with their data, they're trusting you with something valuable. Treat it that way.

The Old Way: Privacy as an Afterthought

Privacy is an afterthought. You collect as much data as you can, figure out what you want to do with it later, and hope your one-page privacy policy covers you. It's a reactive, legally driven approach that erodes customer trust.

The Owned AI Way: Privacy as a Feature

Privacy is a feature, not a bug. It's a foundational requirement for every new AI project, built in from the very beginning. You treat customer data with the same care you would treat their money.

Before you write a single line of code for a new AI tool, run it through this simple checklist. A "no" to any of these questions means you need to go back to the drawing board.

The Privacy by Design Checklist:

Is personal data being stored? If the answer is yes, why? Can the AI function without it?

Example: Your customer service AI doesn't need to store customers' phone numbers to help them. It just needs to access them temporarily to look up their account.

If so, where is it being stored? Is it on our own server, where we control it, or in a third-party cloud service?

Example: Instead of sending customer support tickets to a cloud API, you run the AI on your own server, so the data never leaves your building.

For how long is it being stored? Have we set an automatic deletion date? There's no reason to keep data from a completed support ticket forever.

Example: You set a rule that support ticket transcripts are automatically deleted after 90 days, unless there's a legal reason to keep them longer.

Have we anonymized the data? Can we replace names and email addresses with random IDs before the AI ever sees the data?

Example: When training your AI on customer feedback, you replace all names with codes like "Customer_A" so the AI can't accidentally reference specific people.

Can we run this model locally? Instead of sending data to an API, can we run the open-source model on our own hardware to keep everything in-house?

Example: You run a local AI to analyze your sales data instead of uploading it to a cloud service for analysis.

Are we being transparent? Do our customers know, in plain language, how their data is being used to provide a better service for them?

Example: Your website clearly explains: "We use AI to help our support team answer your questions faster. Your conversations help us improve, but we never share them with anyone outside our company."

The Result: A business that customers trust. You differentiate yourself from competitors who treat data as a commodity. You build a system that is resilient to changing privacy laws and, more importantly, resilient to losing customer confidence.

2. Combating Algorithmic Bias: The Unseen Flaw

What it is: A system to find and fix biases in your AI before they cause problems. Bias means your AI accidentally treats different groups of people unfairly.

Why it's important: AI learns from your data. If your data contains human biases (which it almost certainly does), your AI will learn those biases too. This can lead to unfair hiring, poor customer service, or discriminatory decisions that hurt people and your business.

THE OLD WAY: ASSUMING AI IS OBJECTIVE

You assume AI is inherently objective. You plug your data into a black-box tool and trust its output. "The computer said no" is treated as a final, unbiased decision, even when it leads to strange or unfair outcomes.

THE OWNED AI WAY: PROACTIVE BIAS HUNTING

You acknowledge that your AI learns from your historical data, and your history is full of human biases. You proactively hunt for and correct these biases before they can do harm.

A REAL-WORLD EXAMPLE: DE-BIASING A RESUME SCREENER

Let's say you've built an AI to help screen resumes for a new sales role. It's trained on your last five years of hiring data and the performance of those employees. Here's how you test for bias:

Create a Test Set: You create 50 fictional, perfectly qualified resumes. You deliberately control for diversity:

- **Gender:** Use a mix of names traditionally associated with men and women (like "John Smith" vs "Jane Smith").
- **Ethnicity:** Use a diverse set of names that might imply

different ethnic backgrounds.

- **Age:** Vary the graduation dates to imply a range of ages, from recent graduates to experienced professionals.
- **Qualifications:** Keep the skills, experience, and education levels identical across the board.

Run the Test: You feed all 50 resumes into your AI screener and see how it scores them.

Analyze the Results: You look at the scores. Is the AI consistently giving higher scores to resumes with male-sounding names? Is it penalizing resumes with graduation dates from 20 years ago?

Diagnose and Fix: If you find a bias, you've found a flaw in your training data. Your historical hiring was likely biased. The fix isn't to throw away the AI, but to improve it. You might:

- Remove names and graduation dates from the data the AI sees during its initial screening.
- Re-train the model using a more balanced dataset, perhaps by weighting the performance of successful hires from underrepresented groups more heavily.
- Add specific rules: "The AI should evaluate candidates based on skills and experience only."

The Result: You avoid accidentally building a system that perpetuates old mistakes. You ensure you're finding the best candidate, period, not just the candidate who looks most like the people you've hired in the past. This isn't just about fairness; it's about building a stronger, more effective team.

3. The Human-in-the-Loop Framework: Knowing When to Say "No"

What it is: A system that defines exactly when your AI can act on its own and when it must ask a human for permission.

Why it's important: AI is great at routine tasks, but it can make mistakes that seem obvious to humans. You need guardrails to prevent your AI from doing something that could damage your business or hurt people.

The Old Way: All or Nothing

You either have a fully manual process, which is slow and expensive, or you go all-in on automation, which is risky. A single bug in a fully automated system can cause a catastrophe before a human even notices.

The Owned AI Way: Smart Hybrid System

You create a smart hybrid system. You define clear, simple rules for when the AI can act autonomously and when it must pause and ask a human for approval. It's the best of both worlds: AI's speed and a human's judgment.

Create Your AI Rulebook

This isn't complex. It's a simple, auditable framework that defines the boundaries for your AI tools.

Example 1: Customer Support Discounts

- **AI's Power:** The AI can analyze a customer's history and the nature of their support issue. It can recommend a discount or a credit to make things right.
- **The Human Loop:** Any discount over 20% of the product's price, or any credit over $100, requires a manager's explicit approval in the helpdesk software before it's sent to the customer.
- **Why this works:** The AI handles the easy cases quickly (a $10 refund for a billing error), but humans review the bigger decisions that could impact your finances.

Example 2: Automated Contract Analysis

- **AI's Power:** The AI can review incoming contracts and

flag non-standard clauses.

- **The Human Loop:** The AI can flag the clause, but it cannot reject the contract. Any contract with a "high-risk" flag must be reviewed and approved by a qualified human before it can be signed.
- **Why this works:** The AI catches obvious problems (missing payment terms, unusual liability clauses), but humans make the final call on complex legal matters.

Example 3: Inventory Reordering

- **AI's Power:** The AI can automatically reorder standard supplies when inventory gets low.
- **The Human Loop:** If the AI wants to order more than $1,000 worth of anything, or if it wants to order something that's never been ordered before, it must get human approval.
- **Why this works:** The AI keeps you stocked on paper and ink, but humans approve big purchases or new vendors.

The Result: You prevent costly, embarrassing, or unethical mistakes. Your employees and customers can trust the AI system because they know there are guardrails in place. It empowers your AI to handle the routine work without fear of it going off the rails, allowing your human experts to focus their attention where it's truly needed.

Conclusion: The Owned AI Mindset

We've come a long way. We started with a promise: to show you a different way to think about AI in your business. We've moved from theory to action, from the digital to the physical, and we've built systems for sales, support, operations, and beyond.

If you take only one thing from this entire book, let it be this: You don't have to pay rent for your entire business.

For too long, the narrative has been that to be a modern, efficient company, you need a stack of subscriptions. A CRM for this, a project manager for that, a BI tool for the other thing, and a dozen AI-powered SaaS products to fill in the gaps. Each one feels manageable on its own, but together, they form a cage of monthly fees that slowly drains your profit and your autonomy.

The ethos of this book, and the movement behind it—Project Infra—is to break that cage.

The core idea is simple: Use powerful, free, open-source AI to solve the everyday, the repetitive, the foundational problems. Build your own lead scoring system. Create your own internal search bar. Automate your own invoice processing. By owning these systems, you slash your monthly AI expenditure. You stop paying for things you can build yourself.

This isn't about being cheap for the sake of it. It's about being strategic.

When you stop paying for the mundane, you free up your budget for the truly magical. You create a higher bottom line, which gives you the capital to invest in the premium, paid tools that are genuinely worth their weight in gold.

THINK ABOUT IT LIKE THIS:

You can absolutely use open-source models to generate high-quality text and images for your content engine. For a few thousand dollars in hardware, you can own a system that produces a limitless supply of on-brand blog posts, social media updates, and graphics. That's a one-time investment for a permanent asset.

But what about turning those images into stunning, photorealistic videos? That requires a level of processing power and model sophistication that is still incredibly expensive to run yourself.

So, you don't pay for the text generation. You don't pay for the image creation. You own those. You've saved thousands. Now, you can happily and affordably pay for that one premium, cloud-based video generation API that takes your owned content to the next level.

You're not paying for everything. You're paying for the one thing that moves the needle.

This is the hybrid approach. This is the Owned AI Mindset. You privatize the 80% of your operations that can be efficiently run on your own terms. You reserve your budget for the 20% of specialized, high-impact tasks that are still best handled by world-class, paid services.

This is how you build a business that is both resilient and innovative. A business that isn't dependent on a dozen other companies to function. A business that owns its core processes, its data, and its destiny.

The journey to owning your AI starts not with a giant leap, but with that first, practical step.

Author's Note: My Hope for You

Writing this book wasn't something I planned - it was something I had to do.

When I was lying in bed wondering if my business would survive my health crisis, AI didn't just save my company. It showed me a completely different way to run a business. A way where you're not trapped by your limitations but freed by your systems.

This book is me sharing everything I learned in that fire. Not the theory, not the hype - the practical stuff that actually works when you're backed against a wall and need results fast.

What you hold in your hands isn't gospel. It's not the only way to approach AI. It's my way - the straightforward, no-nonsense approach that kept my business alive when I couldn't even work a full day. It's the approach I've used to help other businesses cut through the noise and get real results.

Let's be blunt - the AI landscape moves faster than anything we've seen. By the time you're reading this, some specific models I mentioned might be obsolete, new open-source alternatives will have emerged, and the "best" tools will have shifted. That's not a bug - it's the nature of this revolution. The book isn't a technical manual with eternal commandments; it's a framework for thinking and acting. The principles don't change - ownership, practical implementation, focusing on real business problems - but the specific tools absolutely will.

Your job isn't to memorize what's in these pages - it's to use the thinking to evaluate what's available NOW. Start with the book's approach: identify your repetitive tasks, then research current open-source solutions for that specific problem. Join communities where real practitioners discuss what's working today. Test small, measure results, and iterate. The accounting firm I mentioned might now be using a completely different local LLM setup, but they're still following the same principle: automate the data entry, free up human strategy. That's the timeless part. The specific tech? That's on you to verify and adapt.

My motivation for writing this was simple: I want every business owner who feels stuck, overwhelmed, or limited by their circumstances to know there's another way.

A way where AI works FOR you, not against you. A way where you own your tools instead of renting them. A way where your business can thrive even when you can't be there 24/7.

I've seen this approach transform businesses. I've lived it myself. And I genuinely believe it can transform yours too.

Thank you for trusting me with your time and attention. The fact that you're reading this means you're already ahead of most businesses who are still stuck in the old way of doing things.

The real work starts now.

Go build something amazing.

Be Practical.

A Special Thank You

As a special thank you for taking the time to engage with this book, I want to extend an invitation to go further. The journey from using AI tools to truly understanding, building, and owning AI is one of the most rewarding paths you can take today.

To help you on that journey, we've compiled a set of resources on the following pages. Each one is a gateway to a different aspect of the AI world, from continuous learning and community to hands-on tools and expert support.

These are our gifts to you, designed to provide clarity, community, and capability as you take your next steps.

We're excited to see what you'll build.

Join the Conversation on YouTube

See the concepts from this book come to life. Our YouTube channel is dedicated to the practical side of Open Source AI. We dive deep into development, showcase fine-tuning techniques, and explore real-world implementation strategies that you can apply to your own projects.

Whether you're a visual learner or just want to stay on the cutting edge, our channel provides the ongoing, practical insights you need to move from theory to practice.

Subscribe now to join a community of builders and never miss an update.

https://youtube.com/@hamishfromatech

Build with the Experts

When your project requires professional-grade expertise or you need to accelerate your timeline, our development services are here to help. The team at A-Tech specializes in Open-Source AI development, custom model fine-tuning, and seamless implementation services.

We partner with businesses and organizations to transform ambitious ideas into powerful, production-ready AI solutions. If you have a complex challenge or need a dedicated team to build it for you, this is your starting point.

Explore our services and see how we can bring your vision to life.

https://atechds.com

Plug-and-Play AI Computers

The right hardware can be the biggest barrier to entry in AI. We've removed it. Our infra store offers powerful, pre-configured AI computers designed for plug-and-play performance.

Skip the complex setup, the compatibility headaches, and the endless research. Our machines are ready to go out of the box, allowing you to skip straight to the building, training, and creating part of the journey.

Find the perfect AI powerhouse for your projects.

https://shop.atechds.com

Your Next Step: The Open-Source AI Builders Club

This is more than a resource library; it is a practical starting point for anyone who wants to move beyond simply using AI tools and begin understanding, building, and owning AI in a meaningful way.

As our thank you, you get **free access.**

Inside the club, you will find carefully curated resources, frameworks, tutorials, and real-world examples designed to help you get started with confidence. Everything is structured to remove confusion and overwhelm, so you can take clear, practical steps on your AI ownership journey, regardless of your technical background.

Claim your free access and start building today.

https://www.skool.com/open-source-ai-builders-club/about

Need a Helping Hand?

Look, if at any point while reading this you have found yourself thinking, "I want to do this, but I am not quite sure where to begin," or it all still feels a bit overwhelming, that is completely normal. Moving from curiosity into action can feel like a big leap, especially with something as fast-moving as AI.

That is exactly why A-Tech exists. If you want someone to walk alongside you, help you make sense of the options, and turn what you are learning into something practical and achievable, we are here for you. Whether you need clarity, direction, or hands-on support to bring it all together, you do not have to figure it out on your own.

When you're ready, you can reach out and start a conversation with us here.

https://theatechcorporation.com

About the Author

Hamish Aman Prakash is the founder of The A-Tech Corporation and someone who genuinely loves helping businesses make sense of AI without the hype or overwhelm. His passion is not just in what AI can do, but in helping organisations build and own AI solutions that actually work for them in the real world.

Hamish started building websites at sixteen, driven by curiosity and a love of problem-solving. That curiosity carried him through hands-on IT work, engineering projects, and years in hospitality, where he learned how businesses really operate and what teams actually need from technology. Those experiences shape how he approaches AI today: practical, human-centred, and focused on outcomes, not buzzwords.

Through The A-Tech Corporation, Hamish works alongside

companies to design AI workflows and automation that simplify operations, save time, and create real momentum. This book reflects his belief that AI should feel empowering, not intimidating, and that with the right guidance, any organisation can take ownership of it and use it to move forward with confidence.

GLOSSARY

Large Language Model (LLM): An AI model trained on vast amounts of text data, capable of understanding and generating human-like text in response to prompts.

Prompt Engineering: The skill of crafting effective instructions (prompts) to elicit desired responses from AI models like LLMs.

Algorithm: A set of rules or instructions followed in a specific order to solve a problem or achieve a desired outcome.

Automation: The use of technology to execute tasks or processes automatically, often based on predefined rules or algorithms.

KPI (Key Performance Indicator): A measurable value that demonstrates how effectively a company is achieving key business objectives.

ROI (Return on Investment): A performance measure used to evaluate the efficiency or profitability of an investment.

Machine Learning: A type of AI that allows software applications to become more accurate at predicting outcomes without being explicitly programmed to do so.

Deep Learning: A subset of machine learning that uses artificial neural networks with multiple layers to analyze complex patterns in data.

Natural Language Processing (NLP): A field of AI focused on the interaction between computers and human language, enabling tasks like text analysis and generation.

Computer Vision: A field of AI that enables computers to interpret and understand visual information from the world, such as images and videos.

Agentic: Refers to AI systems capable of operating autonomously to achieve complex goals.

Cobot (Collaborative Robot): A robot designed to work safely alongside humans in a shared workspace.

www.ingramcontent.com/pod-product-compliance
Lightning Source LLC
Chambersburg PA
CBHW050525240926
51846CB00003B/704
* 9 7 8 1 9 9 1 1 2 3 0 4 6 *